RADIANT BABIES

Connect to Your Baby's Soul

Sharon J. Wesch, Ph.D.

Cover art by LoriAnn Mans and Michio Sano.

First edition 2020.

Publisher:
Sharon J. Wesch, Ph.D.
2235 Whippet Way
Sedona, AZ 86336

TABLE OF CONTENTS

CHAPTER THREE
Healing the Vanishing Twin Syndrome 103

CHAPTER FOUR
Healing Soul Loss after Adoption 165

IN APPRECIATION

My heart is full of deep gratitude. Thank you to all my friends, colleagues, teachers, and students who have supported the birthing of *Radiant Babies.*

I am in profound gratitude to all my courageous clients who agreed to publish their healing experiences in this book. I always teach using stories because they open the heart and bring hope to those who feel lost in their struggle with life's tragedies. It is my intention to describe real-life healing sessions so these descriptions will open the mind of each reader to new possibilities for healing. My sincere hope is that these stories will also touch the soul of each reader—the soul being the deepest level of healing.

I want to thank my editor Raven Dodd. She guided the structure of this book and our many conversations helped me clarify my message to the reader. My appreciation also goes out to the many colleagues who read drafts of the manuscript for clarity and continuity. Their wisdom, insights, and suggestions were invaluable. Thank you to Luann Ditommaso, Al Judge, Betty Ann Dean, Paula Meadows, Malina, Gisele Jolly, and Ann Ramage.

My life has been enriched by the love and support of my soul sisters. They held space, witnessed my journey, and shared their hearts and deep wisdom. So, thank you to Melinda Roeske, Robbin Hartridge, Shannalynne, Holly Schwartztol, Anne King, Janice Vick, and Alice Molter-Serrano.

A special thanks to my friend and soul sister, Denny Reynolds. She recognized the importance of the radiant baby work 20 years ago. She was the first one to say to me, "Your spiritual purpose is to write the book about radiant babies." Every few years she would remind me saying, "You have to write the radiant baby book." Her continuous encouragement has been such a gift.

I especially want to express my gratitude to Marla Sweeney for the information she channeled describing the spiritual purpose of the souls who have volunteered to come to Earth at this time and be born as the radiant babies. The information she brought through from Spirit deepened my understanding of the grand plan that is in place for these special souls.

My life has been enriched by the many spiritual teachers and healers who have assisted me over the past 40 years as I walked the path of spiritual awakening. I am indebted to each of them for helping me evolve to higher levels of consciousness year after year. I feel I must mention one by name. Roy Waite, a spiritual medium from Canada, was the first to show me that spirit babies have the ability to come through the veil and bring messages of hope and healing to their loved ones here on Earth. I consider Roy my professional soul mate. We worked closely together for 10 years bringing healing to so many. He is now on the other side, and I still feel his guidance as I continue the work we once did together.

The beautiful cover for this book was designed by artist, Lori Ann Manns, and graphic designer, Machio Sano. While contemplating the cover for this book Spirit gifted me with the inspiration to place the baby surrounded with Divine Light in the center of a rose. These two gifted artists were able to manifest this idea into the beautiful image you see on the cover. When I first opened the email with this image, it literally took my breath away! My heart is filled with gratitude to both Lori Ann and Michio.

Thank you also to Christiana Gaudet for her support and many hours of spiritual guidance while I was writing this book. Her involvement has been a wonderful blessing. I also want to thank John Gaudet for supervising *Radiant Babies* in the final phases of publishing. He is also responsible for creating my website, Radiant Babies. His contribution is invaluable in distributing this work to the world.

Finally, my heart is full of gratitude to my husband, Dr. Jerry Wesch. We were professional friends and colleagues many years before becoming romantic partners. During those early years he believed in me and opened many doors so I could share Radiant Heart Healing at spiritual conferences across the United States. To this day, he is always there for me, encouraging my healing work and providing the love and support I need to keep moving forward on my spiritual journey. He has been a blessing in my life for over 40 years and I thank Spirit for our deep soul connection.

INTRODUCTION

I invite you, the reader, to consider a soul approach to pregnancy and the prenatal experience. Every baby growing within a mother's womb has both a tiny human body and a magnificent infinite soul. It is the energy of the soul that brings life to the human body. Bringing a precious baby into the world is a sacred event—the miracle of two souls uniting to bring another soul to Planet Earth. Many ancient cultures had spiritual rituals designed to honor the soul of the incoming baby. Sadly, in our modern culture, this is no longer the case; we are no longer attentive to the soul of our incoming babies.

In our modern-day world, we focus on a medical/physical approach to pregnancy. The emphasis is on the physical wellbeing of mother and baby, leaving out any discussion of their spiritual wellbeing. This book makes a case for bringing back a focus on the soul. How do we do this? How do we once again honor the soul of our incoming babies? *Radiant Babies* provides the answer to this very significant question.

What is a Radiant Baby?

Before coming to Earth, the soul of every baby exists in the Universe and is swimming in a sea of Divine Light/Love. I know all souls on the other side are surrounded by Divine Light which generates a feeling of Divine Love within the human heart. We *see* the Divine Light and simultaneously we *feel* the Divine Love. The two happen in a split second; so, I use the term Divine Light/Love. Expectant parents can learn to fill the mother's womb with the energy of Divine Light/Love and thus create the same blissful environment for their baby here on Earth. These babies are born radiant, meaning their precious little hearts are filled with a luminous spirit light that shines out to the world. These special beings never lose their connection to the divine. They are born spiritually awake, and they are born radiant! Imagine a future in which the majority of babies are born radiant. Their ability to bring spiritual love to humankind will transform our world.

Babies Born with Prenatal Wounding

At this time in our evolution, most babies are *not* born radiant. Instead, they are too often born to parents who themselves have wounded hearts; struggle with feeling unloved, and feel no connection to the energy of Divine Light/Love. Given these circumstances, babies experience some form of prenatal emotional wounding because the mother's womb is filled with the dense energy of negative human emotions. These babies are born disconnected from Divine Light/Love and spend their earthly lives, feeling a sense of pervasive emptiness. They are hungry for love and searching for love; yet, their hearts are closed to receiving love. Some of these babies eventually experience the miracle of spiritual awakening and are then reconnected to the Divine Light/Love. Most, however, do not awaken. These babies grow into adults who go to their graves believing they are merely human and are all alone in this painful world of human suffering.

Babies in the womb are conscious beings because their souls are present. They know at a deep level whether they are wanted or unwanted—loved or unloved. The unwanted, unloved babies become emotionally wounded during the prenatal period, and this emotional trauma sets the stage for life-long suffering. This misery can include anxiety, depression, low self-esteem, addictions, suicidal issues, and more. Since all this is happening at an unconscious level, adults suffering from prenatal wounding know something is desperately wrong, but don't know how to identify the problem or heal it.

You might be thinking, "I don't remember any of this." Of course, you don't remember your prenatal experience or your prenatal emotional wounds. All of this is stored in your unconscious mind. Professionals in prenatal psychology believe your prenatal decisions and your stored emotional pain absolutely do affect your thoughts, feelings, and behaviors as an adult. **Your prenatal decisions and your stored emotional pain control you as long as they are unconscious. Bring them to consciousness, and you can shift them!**

Three different situations create prenatal wounding: 1) Babies who were unwanted and/or unloved, 2) Babies placed for adoption, and 3) Babies who had a vanishing twin in the womb. The first two are known and understood. The term vanishing twin needs an explanation. Sometimes a pregnancy starts with two embryos, and then one of the embryos simply vanishes. This event has been medically documented for years using ultrasound technology. As an adult, the surviving twin then suffers from the Vanishing Twin Syndrome. Some of the emotional issues include unexplained grief, anger, depression, anxiety, and a life-long search for *something that is missing.*

The purpose of this book is to educate people about prenatal wounding and also to demonstrate we can identify it, heal it, and even prevent it. Heart-felt client stories presented in this book show the depth of human suffering created by prenatal wounding.

These stories of the heart also show an infusion of Divine Light/ Love creates the miracle of healing and returns these wounded adults to their natural state of radiance.

Using Radiant Heart Healing

The client stories in this book also demonstrate the effectiveness of using a unique spiritual healing modality to alleviate the emotional pain of prenatal wounding. Spirit gifted me this special healing modality in 1984, and I named it Radiant Heart Healing. This modality includes 3 steps: 1) Release the energy of stored emotional pain from the cells of the body. 2) Fill the person's heart with the healing energy of Divine Light/Love. 3) Hold the intention the client will experience a major shift in consciousness. The key to Radiant Heart Healing is the transference of Divine Love into the client's heart. (See Appendix A for a more detailed description of Radiant Heart Healing.) These true stories, collected from over 40 years of doing this work, repeatedly demonstrate Radiant Heart Healing as a very effective tool for healing prenatal wounding.

Radiant Heart Healing is also an effective tool for preventing prenatal wounding. I teach mothers/fathers to fill the mother's womb with the energy of Divine Light/Love. It is best for the parents to do this before conception or in the earliest months of the pregnancy. This spiritual process of filling the womb with Divine Light/Love provides a nurturing environment for the developing babies during the nine months of gestation. These babies feel *at home* because they are in the womb yet surrounded by the Light of Heaven. These babies do not experience a disconnection from the Divine and they do not experience prenatal wounding. They are born radiant.

The Radiant Babies Come with a Spiritual Purpose

The radiant babies are our hope for the future of Planet Earth. Many incoming souls have volunteered to be the radiant babies. We are at a time of spiritual evolution. Radiant babies are born spiritually awake and therefore bring a higher consciousness to our planet. They come in without a veil between their human consciousness and their soul consciousness. They feel one with everything on the planet. These babies know they are here to raise the frequency of Planet Earth and fill the world with Divine Light/ Love. Their spiritual purpose is to create a world that is peaceful, loving, and harmonious. These radiant babies show us how to create Heaven on Earth.

CHAPTER ONE

BRINGING IN RADIANT BABIES

It is My Soul Mission to Bring in Radiant Babies

Everyone comes to Earth with a soul mission. Some people are conscious of their mission; others are not. How do you discover your soul's mission? It usually comes in on the wings of Spirit. It can come as a vision or a message. Often it's quite a surprise. Your soul's mission keeps evolving as you move forward in life and raise your vibratory frequency by bringing more Divine Light and Divine Love into your being.

In the nineteen-nineties I brought Roy Waite, a Canadian spiritual medium, to my home in Indiana. He provided readings for my clients. He used to tell me routinely, "Your spirit guides want me to tell you that you are here to work with children." Each time I would laugh and say to Roy, "I don't do kids." He would shake his head and reply, "Mark my words! You are here to work with children." This went on for years. I didn't believe a word of it.

Years later, I felt guided to write a book about healing grief when a baby dies. Every healing story included the spirit baby coming back and giving healing messages to the grieving family members. I had so many stories. The one book became two books;

Connected for All Time: Book One and Book Two. While struggling to finish those books, I felt inspired to take a trip to Sedona, Arizona.

At the time I was living in Phoenix, Arizona so it was an easy drive to Sedona. I invited a friend and the two of us headed up I-17 towards this magical place. Our intention was to spend some time in meditation on Bell Rock. This rather famous place is called an energy vortex because it is filled with high frequency energy that makes it easier to have mystical experiences. It is said the veil between the earthly world and the spiritual world is very thin at Bell Rock. Just being in the energy of this special place forges a deeper connection to the sacred. Our journey to Sedona was planned with this specific purpose in mind.

We parked the car and began walking toward the majestic red rock formed in the shape of a bell. My attention was immediately drawn to a Native American man walking ten paces ahead of us with a very large drum strapped to his back. This drum reached from the back of his head to the back of his knees—it was just amazing! He was dressed in traditional Native American attire, and a long black braid fell over the drum. Surprisingly, I felt a strong magnetic pull connecting me to this stranger though I had no earthly idea why. At first sight, I wanted to run over to him and start a conversation, but I hesitated because a woman companion walked beside him. The two of them disappeared down a path to the right side of Bell Rock. I assumed they came to do some healing work and would not appreciate the company of a stranger.

With great anticipation, my friend and I hiked up a path on the left side of Bell Rock. We both wanted to keep to the lower levels of this majestic formation. We each found a little niche where we could sit comfortably leaning against the ancient red rocks. Within minutes the earth began to reverberate with the sound of the Indian drum. The hypnotic ancient rhythms were enhanced by the exquisite sounds of a flute.

The music was magical! I felt myself sink into the energy of this spiritual place, leave my everyday thoughts and concerns behind, and drift into the world of Spirit. I remember thinking: *The Universe is giving me the gift of my own private vision quest.* My heart opened to the awesome knowing Spirit was blessing me. Tears of joy and gratitude flowed down my face.

My focus went to the half-finished manuscript for my book about healing grief after the death of an infant. I was stuck in the writing process and wanted it to start flowing again. From my heart, I asked Spirit for assistance. *Show me how to do this. How can I best help grieving loved ones understand their baby is now a spirit? How can I get my message out to the world?* Then I was given this vision—it was like daydreaming.

I saw my spirit-self walking like the Pied Piper with hundreds of spirit babies following me as I moved from this world into the afterlife. There was no grief or sadness as we flowed easily along with a sense of great purpose. We all simply slipped through an opening in the clouds and disappeared from sight. These important words came unbidden. *This is your soul mission. You are here to connect the spirit babies with their grieving loved ones. There is no death. There is only love. Take this message to the world.*

The vision faded and all was quiet for a few moments. My attention was captured once again by the melodious flute music as it danced with the rhythm of the drum. The vibration of the ancient music filled every cell of my body and carried me once again into the world of Spirit. The visions continued with more scenes that touched my heart so deeply I could hardly breathe. Once again, I saw my spirit-self walking like the Pied Piper with hundreds of spirit babies following me. However, this time I was bringing the babies from their place in the light and leading them through the clouds to Planet Earth. More words flowed into my consciousness. *This too is your soul's mission. You are here to bring these spirit babies to the Earth plane. These spirits will be radiant babies. You are here to open the portal.* Immediately, I was surrounded with this blinding Divine Light. My heart opened, and I felt the truth of these words fill my heart with Divine Love. I have no idea how much time passed before I came back to an awareness of this Earth.

This spontaneous vision quest with the drums and the flute music was one of those synchronistic events that could only have been arranged by Spirit. It was truly a God-moment. I've held the vision of bringing radiant babies to Earth for 15 years. Now is the time to bring it forward. The time is now because humanity has shifted to a higher consciousness, and more people will open their hearts and minds to the spiritual wisdom presented in this book. Spirit tells me the world is ready for bringing in radiant babies.

The Radiant Baby Process is About Birthing the Soul of Each Infant

Before conception the baby's soul existed on the other side of the veil in an environment of pure light which is the energy of Divine Love. This Divine Love is the highest frequency possible. It is much different than the lower frequency energies of the Earth plane. Sending the energy of Divine Love into the mother's womb allows the baby's soul to exist here on Earth and still be floating in the same high frequency energies that surrounded this soul while in the spiritual world. While still in the womb, each baby is then enveloped in Divine Love and does not experience the usual disconnection from the Divine. Each baby is born with Divine Love flowing into their heart and making a big bright aura around the baby's tiny physical body. Through this process, each baby is born radiant!

Traditionally, prenatal classes focus on the physical health of mother and baby—nutrition, Lamaze training for assistance with labor and delivery, and information about nursing the baby. In our modern medical model, we have become so focused on the physical body and the human level of existence that we have forgotten to attend to the soul. The Radiant Baby Process is a paradigm shift to a more spiritual way of bringing babies into the world. This new way is focused on birthing the soul of each infant.

In the center of every baby's heart is a spark of God-energy. The Radiant Baby Process teaches parents and others to acknowledge this divine spark and visualize sending the energy of Divine Light into the mother's womb. The Divine Light ignites the spark of God-energy, making a big ball of Divine Light within the baby's heart center. While the baby is still in the womb, clairvoyants can actually "see" this heart-light shining within the mother's abdomen. This Divine Light also expands the baby's energy field making a bright light around the baby. When the baby is born, all this spiritual energy shines from within, lighting up the baby's eyes and smile. There's an old saying, "The eyes are the windows to the soul." Indeed, the light of the soul shines forth through the eyes of each precious radiant baby.

This spiritual light is the catalyst for all human beings to awaken to the presence of Spirit. These babies are here to shift the consciousness of the world, and awaken those who are spiritually asleep. When this happens, humankind will evolve to higher levels of consciousness and be able to create Heaven on Earth. I trust this will happen because it is all meant to be.

The following stories describe my work of bringing in radiant babies. I have a deep knowing the parents in these stories were guided by Spirit to find me and learn this process of birthing the soul. Remember, from the spiritual point of view, there are no accidents. The events in these stories were divinely orchestrated so each incoming baby could be born radiant.

Birthing the First Radiant Baby

Spirit has led me to many places and provided so many gifts on my spiritual journey of developing Radiant Heart Healing. The gift of birthing radiant babies has been one of my greatest treasures. It all began with one client named Marie.

Marie originally came to my holistic clinic in Northwest Indiana seeking information and techniques to become more assertive at work. She felt she was having difficulty communicating with other professionals in her job as a hospital nurse. Indeed, she did need assertiveness training, but we also uncovered a much deeper psychological trauma as her therapy proceeded.

The first thing I noticed about Marie was her extreme avoidance of being touched. My usual style is to hug my clients at the end of each session. Marie would not allow me to hug her, nor did she allow anyone else to touch her in any way. After several months of individual sessions, she participated in a weekly therapy group. She was careful to avoid being touched by anyone in the group and darted for the door when other group members exchanged good-bye hugs.

I thought this behavior was rather strange for a thirty-five-year-old woman. I immediately suspected sexual abuse as the core reason for her defensiveness; indeed, this is what eventually surfaced. Marie gradually became strong enough psychologically to allow the repressed memories of childhood sexual abuse to emerge from the secret files of her unconscious. The memories that surfaced over a period of six months were the worst I'd heard in all my years of practicing psychotherapy. She opened to the memory of her minister grandfather abusing her on the church altar at the age of three. Her adult body still carries the scars of being physically ripped and torn during this episode. Before our work together, her heart still carried the emotional scars of this horrific abuse.

A major part of our work was aimed at healing her heart. It was obvious to me she had closed off her heart to protect herself from the devastating emotional pain. I assured her this was a wise decision because these feelings were too much for any child to bear. Now that she was in therapy, she could choose to open her heart and release the pain, hurt, and sadness of the betrayal by her grand-father. She did much deep work releasing the emotional pain she had carried for thirty years. I could feel the energy of it come out of the cells of her body, releasing the energy blocks she created at the time of the abuse. She showed great courage in her willingness to do the release work. Her heart began to heal, and she opened a tiny bit to connecting with other members of the therapy group.

Marie's healing process went on for months; towards the end she discovered she was pregnant. Initially, she was shocked because she and her husband John had both agreed they did not ever want to have a child. They had been married for sixteen years in a very stable but emotionally detached relationship.

Marie adapted rather quickly to the idea of being pregnant. Within the first weeks she even saw the baby as an unexpected blessing. However, her husband had much greater difficulty ad-justing to this turn of events. He was extremely angry and seri-ously tried convincing Marie to have an abortion. Of course, he was responding from his own woundedness. However, he was not conscious of the psychological issues preventing him welcoming this new baby into the family. Marie resisted his pressures and de-cided to keep the baby. She knew in her heart she couldn't allow any other choice. She had already bonded heart-to-heart with this new life she carried within her body.

John reluctantly entered therapy for himself to come to terms with the prospect of becoming a father. He expressed many deep feelings about the pregnancy, including rage at the prospect of rais-ing a child. Actually, his rage was covering deep fears and feelings of inadequacy regarding parenting this new human being. He had very negative memories of his own childhood in a severely dysfunc-tional family. He had developed a closed heart to hide the emo-tional pain he felt about feeling unloved and emotionally abused by his parents. He also felt deeply jealous about the prospect of sharing his wife's time and attention with a new baby. Gradually he came to understand these feelings were the result of his own early childhood needs being unmet. He also came to realize he could change his feelings by doing his own psychotherapy and making his own shifts in consciousness. I remember saying to both of them:

> "This baby is going to be a little miracle baby;
> and the miracle will be the transformation of each of you."

Marie and John spent the last six months of the pregnancy preparing for the birth. They read books on parenting and child development, listened to tapes, took Lamaze classes, and reorganized the house to allow for a baby's room. Marie came to my office for weekly healing sessions. Together we did the imagery to fill her heart with Divine Light and then send it to this precious baby in her womb. We also talked to the baby sending messages of Divine Love. John sometimes joined us so he could also participate in sending the Divine Light and adding his voice to the process of sending love messages to the baby.

It was Christmas time, and I went shopping for Christmas gifts on my lunch hour. Spirit guided me to a spiritual bookstore near my clinic where I found an audio tape by Dawson Church entitled, "Communicating with the Soul of Your Unborn Child." I felt this burst of joy in my heart when I saw the title. Without even listening to the tape, I knew it was the perfect gift for John, Marie, and their baby. The timing was perfect. They were coming in for a session in just a few hours. As I drove back to my office, I heard a little voice in my head say, *God works in strange and wondrous ways.*

The tape contained a whole series of guided imagery exercises designed to bond the soul of the baby with the souls of the parents. It also had imagery designed to open the hearts of both parents and connect their hearts energetically with the baby's heart. John and Marie took the tape with them on a trip to Hawaii where they practiced the visualizations daily as they vacationed in this beautiful island paradise.

John had a transformational experience while he and Marie were listening to the tape in a beautiful garden setting in Hawaii. He described it with a look of wonder in his eyes.

> It was a cloudy overcast day, and we were sitting on the lawn of our vacation house. We were going through the process and were just at the part that says, "Put your hand on the fetus and send loving energy to this new soul." As I did this, the clouds opened up and a stream of bright light poured forth shining right on the three of us. It was a very magical moment for me. Something shifted in me, and I felt different about the baby from that moment on. I know I opened my heart in that moment and bonded with our unborn child that I had been rejecting.

This was a transformational moment for John. I was so thankful to the Universe for helping him achieve this shift in consciousness. Now, he could truly be the father this baby needed in order to be born into love. Now, he could open his heart to this infant and give the loving energy needed for a wonderful beginning. Without this shift in consciousness, he would have only been going through the motions, and the baby would sense he was faking it.

The last month before the birth, Marie became quite agitated and fearful about the labor and delivery process. She began having recurring nightmares about her childhood sexual abuse scenes. The impending birth seemed to be stirring up the remains of the buried emotional pain from her childhood abuse. I became quite concerned for her psychological well-being during the painful process of labor and delivery. I actually feared she might experience a psychotic break if the labor and delivery pain was too reminiscent of the earlier pain of her abuse. She spent several weeks doing fear release work in an attempt to totally clear herself of the old trauma.

My heart went out to her at the end of one particularly intense session. I asked if she wanted me to assist her during the birth process. She burst into sobs and hugged me holding on like a very frightened child. She gave me an immediate yes.

At the time, we thought we had three weeks until the birth. Marie's obstetrician listened to the circumstances and agreed to allow me in the labor and delivery room. We also scheduled an appointment that same afternoon for me to meet with John and Marie together. The three of us spent the hour discussing the preventative measures I felt were necessary for Marie's psychological well-being.

The very next night, my home phone rang at 10 p.m. It was John saying Marie was in labor, and they were leaving for the hospital. He asked me to arrive at midnight. I agreed and promptly broke out in a cold sweat from a panic attack. Suddenly, I realized I had no earthly idea what I needed to do to assist in this process. I had volunteered the day before from my heart. My mind had not had time to formulate a plan of action. However, I trusted my intuition and my heart, knowing I needed to be present.

I marveled at how everything had fallen into place easily the day before. I thought it was an interesting bit of synchronicity that Marie did her feeling release work in the morning, received her doctor's approval in the afternoon, and then found an empty hour on my schedule for their couple's session. It all flowed smoothly and without effort as if we all knew the birth was imminent. As I drove to the hospital, I talked to myself. *You are not alone in this. You have a lot of guidance. Listen to your guides. They will help you know what to do.*

When I arrived at the labor room, Marie was doing very well. She had taped a picture on the wall next to her bed. I felt my heart open as I looked at this picture. It was a mother's hand reaching out to an infant who was grasping her thumb with precious little fingers. A white light streamed from the mother's hand into the hand of the baby. The light seemed to be connecting them and surrounding their hands in a wonderful glow.

Marie had intuitively found a wonderful symbol of all the energy work we had practiced over the previous months. The caption on the picture stated, "Touching: One of your baby's greatest needs." As I looked at this picture through the long night, I silently thanked Marie for her inspiration to seek treatment several years before the birth of this baby. Now that she had made her shifts in consciousness, she could truly touch this baby with her loving energy from an open heart. Though they had not yet touched on the physical level, I knew she had already touched this baby's soul.

John and Marie had taken Lamaze childbirth training. As her labor pains increased, John coached her in breathing through the pain. They were quite connected emotionally as they worked together to birth this baby. John stood at the side of her bed holding her hand and talking her through each contraction. I chose a place on the other side of Marie, being careful not to interfere in the bonding between them. I induced a deep state of relaxation and began giving Marie calming suggestions designed to help her relax and flow with the process while reducing her fear and her physical pain. John followed my lead and repeated some of the same suggestions.

The labor lasted approximately six hours, which was very fast for a first-time delivery. I used the following imagery to assist Marie in relieving her labor pains:

See yourself floating on a pink cloud. Allow your body to sink into the softness of the pink energy.

Send any pain you have into the cloud. This wonderful cloud will take away all your pain.

Allow your body to float above the pain as you relax easily and effortlessly on this wonderful cloud.

Without explaining to Marie, I was purposefully using the color pink because it is the color of Divine Love.

These suggestions seemed to help Marie rise above her labor pain. Several hours into the process, I spontaneously added some new suggestions. These must have come from my guidance because I did not consciously plan to say them. It was as if I opened my mouth and suddenly heard myself saying these new hypnotic suggestions. They flowed easily and effortlessly as if I had written a script and rehearsed it. I heard myself saying:

> With each contraction, your heart opens to receive this baby in love.
> As your cervix opens for the delivery, your heart opens to bond energetically with this baby.
>
> Your heart is more and more open to receive this baby in love.
> As your cervix dilates, your heart chakra opens in equal proportions.
>
> Visualize opening your heart and sending love energy into this child as you hold her against your heart. Surround the two of you in a pink bubble of Divine love.

As I continued through the night with these suggestions, Marie stayed rather calm and peaceful, rising above the pain and proceeding with the labor process without any psychological problems. At times throughout the night, I placed my own hand on her chest and sent healing energy into her heart. I found I could easily keep visualizing and sending healing energy into Marie's heart while I verbally sent the messages for pain relief and opening her heart. I also felt my own heart opening and being filled with radiant energy as I worked as a channel for Marie.

As I held a loving presence for this couple, I silently asked God and Mother Mary to bless this mother, baby, and father. I silently asked that the radiant healing energy be guided to heal all their hearts so they would be open and clear for the heart bonding to happen with grace and ease.

Throughout the process, Marie's doctor and nurses were very cooperative. They had no concept of what I was doing by sending the healing energy into Marie's heart, but they could see Marie was very calm and doing extremely well both physically and psychologically. I felt encouraged because they allowed the process to continue and did not make any negative comments that might have interrupted the spiritual birthing process.

The final moment of birth is a moment in time that will always remain as a peak experience for me in this lifetime. I felt so honored to be present and witness this wondrous event. At the moment of birth, Marie cried with joy at finally seeing the baby she'd been communicating with for so many months. Her heart was so open her feelings were flowing easily. She was laughing and crying and being absolutely jubilant. Tears flowed down her cheeks as the doctor placed their beautiful baby girl skin-to-skin on Marie's stomach. Marie began spontaneously talking to this new human being:

Welcome to the world little one. I'm your mother and this is your father. We have talked to you for months already. Your name is going to be Katie.

We have waited so long to see you and touch you. And now here you are! We love you so much and are so happy to have you.

Then Marie brought the baby to her heart. John placed his hand on the back of Katie's heart and sent loving energy into her from his own heart. Marie placed both her hands on top of his and together they wrapped this baby in a blanket of love. They did this without any communication with each other or any instruction from me. It was as if they were guided by some unseen and unheard directions that were just perfect.

It was such a magical moment, touching everyone in the room. The doctor, the nurses, John, Marie, and I all cried with our hearts wide open as we witnessed the absolute beauty of this new soul being received into the world with such loving tenderness.

Then the most amazing thing happened as the nurses took the baby to the bassinet beside the bed. Marie, the woman who couldn't be touched, began spontaneously hugging and kissing her husband, the doctor, the nurses, and me. She threw her arms wide open, drew each one of us up against her heart and hugged us each tightly. She even kissed each one of us, joyously calling out, "I love you."

Marie was so open and so loving I was amazed at her transformation. This was not the same woman who had begun treatment three years earlier. I felt like I had witnessed a double miracle. The first miracle was the birth of a new soul in this beautiful baby girl. The second miracle was Marie opening her heart to this baby and then to everyone present in the room. Suddenly, I remembered my words of prophecy to John and Marie at the beginning of her pregnancy: "This baby will be a little miracle baby. And the miracle will be the transformation of each of you." I silently thanked all the unseen forces for being present and helping me to facilitate this transformational process.

Five Years Later

It has been years since the three of us created this wonderful birthing process using the suggestions for opening Marie's heart. As I predicted, this baby is a miracle baby, and she has indeed motivated her parents to advance on their individual healing journeys. They both continued their therapy with the goal of healing their relationship and becoming the best parents possible. They both understand at a very deep level they are preventing the hereditary chain of negative messages from being passed on to another generation. They also both understand the work they are doing is healing future generations.

John recalled these feelings about the birth process:

I had this moment of pure joy when our baby was born. I felt this exhilaration I have never felt before or since. My own heart was wide open being in the presence of such a miracle. Katie is helping me heal my own heart. I'm learning how to love because she came into my life and into my heart. I am warmer and softer now that I have opened my heart. This is the first time in my life I have felt anything in my heart. I guess I am beginning to experience loving with my heart rather than with my head.

I am learning so much from parenting Katie. I have learned to accept another person and give unconditional love. She is also teaching me to feel my feelings. Her feelings are so transparent. She's happy, sad, scared, mad, and she shows it. In a way, she is teaching me how to be open with my own feelings.

Marie said of her daughter:

As a newborn infant Katie was extremely calm, content and peaceful. She slept through the night at six weeks. She rarely cried unless she had a reason. As soon as we met her needs, she would quit crying.

She seems to have a special glow about her. People come up to us in restaurants and shopping malls and remark how special she is. Often people say things like, "She is such a little angel." I think people pick up on her radiant nature.

Spiritual Discussion

I had been working with identifying and healing prenatal wounding for years before this work with Marie and John. Several months before Marie came into my practice, I had an inspired thought flow into my mind while driving home from the clinic one evening. *I know how to identify and heal prenatal wounding so why don't I create a way to prevent it.* I remember thinking this was an inspired idea, and at the same time, I had no earthly idea how to create such a process. I was clueless. So, I put this idea on the back burner and continued to facilitate healing with the clients that Spirit put in front of me each day.

I was so filled with joy when Marie announced she was pregnant. I was joyful for her and this miracle baby developing within her womb. At the same time, I was joyful for myself. I knew Spirit just opened the door for me to begin the work of preventing prenatal wounding. And though I had no clue how to proceed, I trusted I would be guided each step of the way. And I was!

I had the luxury of doing weekly healing sessions with Marie from the moment she knew she was pregnant till the moment she delivered Katie. I also had the luxury of a co-operative father. They both trusted me, so I felt free to try various visualizations for bringing Divine Love energy into this mother's womb. It was a very fun, creative experience with no sense of pressure to make something happen. Marie and I laughed and played together as we sent the Divine Love energy into her womb. Then she would give me feedback about how she felt and how the baby in the womb was responding. Both Marie and John continued practicing these visualizations at home between sessions. Working with them to develop The Radiant Baby Process was such a joy! I felt truly blessed by Spirit.

Anchoring Soul Energy in a Baby's Heart

I was traveling and teaching Radiant Heart Healing in Florida. A client I'll call Laura scheduled a healing session. We discovered she was an unwanted baby who never bonded with her mother. She did a very emotional prenatal healing session with me to clear her prenatal wounding. Because of the work we did in that first session, she left feeling lighter and made a conscious decision she was lovable. Now, a year later, she called for another session because she was three months pregnant. Laura had great anxiety that, like her mother, she would not be able to bond with this precious baby developing within her womb. She was 27 years old at the time of this second session.

I began Laura's healing session with some visualization exercises designed to bring in the higher frequencies of Divine Love. I guided Laura to join me in sending down imaginary roots into the Earth to get grounded and send an imaginary funnel into the heavens to connect with the energy of Divine Love. As these energies merged in her heart, I placed my hand on her chest and began sending more Divine Love energy through my heart, down my arm, out my hand, and into her heart.

While concentrating on doing this energy work, I became aware of a beam of Divine Light coming from the heavens, through the ceiling, and flowing directly into Laura's heart. As it came in, the spiritual energy in her heart intensified greatly. She experienced this as a great warming of her heart.

Dr. Sher: There's a beam of Divine Light coming from the heavens and going directly into your heart. That's all I can think about.

Laura: Yes, I can see it.

Dr. Sher: You can see it? How wonderful! Have you seen light like this before?

Laura: No. This is the first time. It's a yellow stream of light with sparkles in it—sparkles like you see when the sun shines on the water. It's incredibly bright, and it lights up the whole room. And it's making my heart extremely hot.

Dr. Sher: This is a very sacred moment. This is Divine Love coming directly into your heart. Mother Mary is standing directly in front of us. She's the Divine Mother, you know. The light beam is coming through her heart and into yours. She always comes when I do the work with the babies. Can you see Mother Mary?

Laura: No, but I believe she's there. My heart feels expanded, and it's still very hot. I have never felt anything like this before. I feel so peaceful.

Dr. Sher: You are being filled with Divine Love. You deserve this love. You are a precious child of God, and you are very loved. Just keep taking it in.

We both were quiet for a time as we sat in wonder and awe of this sacred moment. There was a bubble of light around both of us, and the whole room was infused with light and a sense of deep peace. It was like being in a sacred place of worship or visiting an ancient spiritual site. We both spoke in hushed tones so as not to disturb the wonder.

Dr. Sher: Now we need to direct this same light into your abdomen, so the baby is surrounded with Divine Love. You can direct energy with your mind. So just imagine that light flowing down from your heart and surrounding your baby nestling in your womb. See it in your mind's eye and it will happen. At the same time, I'm going to put my hands on your abdomen and guide the love energy to flow through me.

Laura: Wow! This is pretty incredible. My whole abdomen is getting as hot as my heart.

Dr. Sher: Good. That's how it's supposed to feel.

Laura: This feels so wonderful!

Dr. Sher: I'm going to talk to your baby. You just keep sending the love energy from your heart to the baby and listen to the messages.

As I began to talk to the baby, the beam of light flowing into Laura's heart faded, and another beam of the same intensity flowed from the heavens into her abdomen. It was something to behold! Laura could feel it immediately, and her abdomen gradually became as warm as her heart. Spirit guided my words as I talked to the baby in the womb:

> You are a beautiful gift from God. You are our precious little one.
> We are so glad you are here. You are surrounded with Divine Love.
>
> You are so lovable. You deserve so much love.
> Your mommy and your daddy love you so much.
>
> They are so glad you chose to come to their family.
> They will love you and support you on your journey here on Earth.
> You are safe. They will take good care of you.
>
> You are a powerful soul in a tiny baby body.
> You came with a purpose, and we are here to assist you in that purpose.

Dr. Sher: Now, Laura, put your hands on your abdomen and imagine sending the love from your heart down your arms, through your hands, and into the baby. Good. Intention is everything. You just have to have the intention, and it works. You are sending from your heart and your hands, and I'm still sending with my hands. Spirit is also assisting as we do this work together.

A look of amazement came over Laura as she experienced the intensity of all this energy coming into her body. Within a few minutes, I felt an energetic shift in Laura's abdomen. It felt like *something moved* under my hands.

Dr. Sher: Did you feel that?

Laura: Yes. I couldn't miss it. It felt like something popped. It was like an expansion of some kind in my abdomen.

Dr. Sher: Exactly. I heard a fascinating message from Spirit. *You just anchored the soul energy in your baby's heart.*

Laura: (laughing and crying) I felt the floodgates of my mother love open. Oh, WOW! I'm going to be a mother!

Dr. Sher: (laughing) Yes, indeed. You already are a mother. Didn't you know?

Laura: Well, yes, but not really. I sort of knew it, but now I feel it. Somehow, it's different.

We continued to send the Divine Love energy through our hands into the baby for another five minutes. Both Laura and I were very quiet as we sat guiding the energy. We were surrounded with such spiritual peace. It was rather like praying together. Mother Mary continued to stand in front of us. The beam of light from the heavens continued to flow through her into Laura's abdomen and the baby. I got the inspired thought Mary was holding open a portal between Heaven and Earth thus creating the opening for the flow of Divine Love. Just as I received this inspiration, I heard a voice in my head.

> *In the center of every baby's heart is a spark of God.*
> *The love energy has fanned this spark of divinity into a huge flame.*
> *This baby will know love. This is how birth is meant to be.*

I answered silently in my thoughts. *Yes, this baby felt Divine Love today. This is a radiant baby!*

My own heart opened, and I felt a wonderous rush of gratitude, joy, and love. Of course, I know I never work alone; so I silently thanked Mother Mary, the angels, my spirit guides, and all the other unseen beings who were present and guiding this healing session.

One Week Later

I interviewed Laura just one week later to ask about any changes she observed since this profound session. She reported:

> From the time I discovered I was pregnant I had a great deal of anxiety. I had questions like: "Am I going to have a closed heart like my mother? Will I reject this baby like I was rejected? Can I overcome that pattern? Can I be an OK mom? How will I know what to do?" Now that's all gone, and I feel completely at ease. Everything is going to be just fine. I now feel peaceful instead of fearful.
>
> Now I also find myself talking to the baby both in my head and out loud as I go about my day. I tell my baby the messages you said during the session. I especially say, "I love you. I'm excited you are here. Your daddy loves you." Sometimes I just talk about what I'm doing at the moment. I just keep chattering away. It's so fun! Different, but fun!
>
> I am so bonded with this baby. I've heard other mothers talk about "falling in love" with their babies at first sight—like in the delivery room. Well, I feel like that already. During our healing session, I had my moment of falling in love with my baby. I think it was when I said the floodgates of my mother love just opened. I will remember that feeling in my heart the rest of my life. It is etched in my memory forever.

The biggest change is with my physical body. From the moment I got pregnant, I've had this terrible morning sickness. I've been throwing up every day, all day, for three months. It's been just horrendous! I've been in bed much of the time. That is 90 % gone. Now I throw up only once a day, maybe twice a week. I can't explain it, but I received this wonderful healing about my morning sickness. What a blessing!

SPIRITUAL DISCUSSION

Like all healers, I am God's instrument and Divine Love flows through me as I do this work with the babies. The Divine Love energy fanned the spark of God into a huge flame in this baby's heart, the mother's heart, and my heart. It all happened in a moment of grace.

As parents, we think we are here to teach our children. That idea is mostly an illusion. In this story we see this powerful soul came to teach her mother about motherly love. The soul of this baby also came to assist me in developing the method for bringing in radiant babies.

You might be wondering about the appearance of Mother Mary in this session. Like many other healers, I am blessed to have the assistance of Mother Mary as I do my healing work. I usually don't see her, but I know she has entered my healing room when I begin thinking about her. She is the essence of mother love, and I can feel her high frequency energy fill the room. I can also feel her inspiration as she guides my thoughts and gives me the exact words each client needs to hear. She always comes when I work with the babies doing the Radiant Baby Process. Clients like Laura, who are clairvoyant, usually see her in the room. Often, she gives my clients direct healing messages or actually participates in the healing session like she did with Laura. I am forever grateful for all the assistance I receive from the Blessed Mother.

I Came to be with My Big Sister

I sometimes teach about radiant babies in a group setting. In fact, this is a much more effective way to get my message out to young parents and health care professionals working with mothers and babies.

Rebecca, another young woman who loves babies, has a passion for teaching natural childbirth classes. This young woman is spiritually awake and brings her spiritual beliefs into her childbirth classes. Rebecca is incredibly psychic and often receives messages from babies in the womb, newborn babies, and even their family pets. One day the family cat was purring loudly while nestled on her chest. Rebecca distinctly heard the cat say, "I love you."

Rebecca convened a small group of expectant parents so I could talk to them about viewing their babies as spiritual beings with important spiritual and emotional needs that are not usually addressed. They all seemed fascinated to hear about radiant babies and easily learned to send Divine Light into their hearts and then out their hands. I loved watching their faces light up as each one awakened to sensing the God-energy.

Don and Chris brought their precious Angela to the class. She was a tiny, cuddly twelve-month-old who obviously knew she was totally loved. This petite little blonde stayed safely nestled in her daddy's arms, flirted coyly with all of us in her innocent baby way, and opened everyone's heart. We could clearly see her soul light shining from within. This light illuminated her little face and her eyes. She was indeed a radiant baby!

Chris was sixteen weeks pregnant with their second child and had just felt the quickening. This baby was a surprise, but Don and Chris adapted quickly, saying, "This baby deserves for us to be as excited as we were about Angela."

I invited Chris to sit in the middle of the circle so we could welcome this new baby with the energy of Divine Love. She jumped at the chance. Chris seemed excited and was extremely open and receptive. She easily took in the love energy from everyone in the circle.

Chris: I'm buzzing! It's all prickly like electricity flowing through me. This is fun!

We each sent a loving verbal message to this new being coming to Earth.

Dr. Sher: You are so loved in this family, and you have a wonderful older sister.

At that very moment, I saw Rebecca's eyes light up with amazement and wonder. She was being quiet, but I intuitively knew something quite significant had just occurred. So, I put her on the spot.

Dr. Sher: Rebecca, I know you just received an intuitive message. Can you share that with us?"

Rebecca: The baby got all excited when Dr. Sher spoke about her older sister. I could see her little spirit jumping around and waving her little hands at me! Then she gave me this message, "I came to be with my sister. She's the reason I'm here."

This message clearly touched this mother's heart and tears of joy flowed down her face. Rebecca said in a hushed tone, "I guess there's a reason for everything. This new baby wanted to grow up with Angela. Obviously, they have a real strong soul connection. I'm so happy to know!"

SPIRITUAL DISCUSSION

There are many healers, psychics, mediums, and Reiki practitioners who report receiving messages from a baby in the womb. It's also quite common for sensitive mothers and grandmothers to receive special messages from an incoming soul before conception and while the baby is developing in the womb. My brother's wife received a message from their first grandchild while this baby was still in the womb. While walking a labyrinth, Grandma Melinda heard very distinctly, "I'm here." Days later her son and his wife stopped by to share, "Guess what! You are going to be grandparents!"

You might be wondering how this can be when the baby in the womb has no brain and no communication skills. Remember, it's not the human part of the baby sending these messages. Rather, it's the spirit of the baby. The spirits of our loved ones can send messages from the other side. Likewise, the spirit of a baby can communicate from the other side before birth and/or while in the womb.

Every Baby Deserves the Gift of Divine Love

When I created the Radiant Baby Process, my own two children were already in their 20s. Of course, my heart hurt knowing I did not send Divine Love to my own womb while I was pregnant with them. I loved them both with a profound mother love—yet I know it was not the same as igniting that spark of Divine Love in their little hearts.

Many mothers have this same response when they learn about radiant babies. They are usually very sad because of their own birth story, and they are also deeply sad for the children they brought into the world. Often, these mothers feel guilty. This seems to be a universal response. Nobody ever taught them about bringing in radiant babies. I always tell them, "You could not do what you didn't know."

There is a solution to the dilemma of mothers who did not form a love connection with their baby. It's called Healing Back in Time. For this healing, I invite the mother to go back in time and imagine she has her baby within her womb. I direct her to see herself at the age she was when she was pregnant with this baby. Then I guide her through the visualizations of bringing Divine Light into her heart and sending this high frequency love energy into her womb. We spend time bathing the developing infant with Divine Light and giving this baby messages about being so loved. I can't explain exactly how it works—I just know it does. Both the mother and the child feel a change. Sometimes, the change is subtle. Other times it is blatant. Either way, it usually creates a healing that is very meaningful.

Sue Creates the Mother-Baby Bond with Her Child

This next story gives evidence Healing Back in Time really does work. Sue, mother of Michael and Megan, gifted me her story for the book.

> I was married and just 20 years old when I discovered I was pregnant the first time. I did not enjoy being pregnant. I must say, it was the longest nine months of my life. Fear about a baby growing inside my body caused me anxiety, and I was panicky about becoming a mother. I was running away from myself and felt very disconnected from my feelings. Expressing what was happening to me emotionally was impossible. I never talked about it, so my husband and my family didn't know. When our beautiful Michael was born, I loved him, but it was in a distant sort of way.

> I still felt no heart-to-heart connection with Michael as he grew. I was in psychotherapy with Dr. Sher for a year when I became pregnant again three years after Michael. I was learning about releasing my fears and other painful feelings and how to replace them with love energy. Dr. Sher taught me how to do relaxation and visualization techniques to calm my anxiety. I also learned ways to get to know and love "who I am". She taught me to open my heart and receive the energy

of Divine Love. Through the Radiant Heart Healing Process, I made a re-decision: "I deserve to be loved." After learning to give and receive love for myself, I could also open my heart to others. My heart now feels full instead of empty.

This second pregnancy was such a different experience for me! Each week Dr. Sher and I sent positive healing energy into my abdomen so the baby would be surrounded in love and light. I could really feel the warm energy all though my belly and it also flowed through the rest of my body. Not only did the baby receive all the "goodies," but so did I. I just loved it! Then Dr. Sher taught my husband and me to do the same thing at home. This time, I spent the nine months of the pregnancy filled with joy and love instead of fear.

I felt bonded with Megan even before she was born. In fact, I have never had such a connection as the one I have with Megan. It seems Megan stored all that love and light inside of her. Right from the start, she seemed to shine. To this day Megan is very confident, loving, relaxed, and at ease with herself. She is joyful, laughs a lot, and seems to enjoy every day of her life.

After feeling this warm bond with Megan, I longed to have the same relationship with Michael. I didn't know how to get it. Dr. Sher guided me through a process called "Healing Back in Time." The goal was for me to bond with Michael when he was a baby in the womb. Dr. Sher said we could do this without Michael being physically present. Together, we sent Divine Love energy (the light) back in time to him as a baby in the womb. I don't understand it, but it worked! I witnessed an immediate and dramatic change in Michael who was four years old at the time. He suddenly became a cuddly little boy, and he attached to me like a magnet. I was overjoyed! Finally, we could really feel a love connection with each other.

Sending Divine Love energy to a baby in the womb is such a gift for your unborn child. It is a wonderful experience and as they grow up, they show you all they received, and they also send it back. Both of my children are so awesome! I'm sure it's because I learned to surround them with Divine Love in the womb. It's such a simple, yet powerful, thing to do. Every baby needs this gift of Divine Love while still in the womb.

SPIRITUAL DISCUSSION

Perhaps you are feeling sad you didn't know about sending Divine Love into your womb when you were pregnant. I invite you to use this healing method, Healing Back in Time. It's really quite simple. Find a quiet place where you can be entirely alone. Play some relaxing spiritual music and create your own healing moment for you and your child. Ask for the assistance of Mother Mary and your guardian angels. Imagine your child is a tiny group of cells developing within your womb. Visualize Divine Light flowing in the top of your head. See it filling all the cells in your head, flowing down into your heart, and then flowing down into your womb to surround your baby in Divine Love. Then talk to your baby from your heart, sending messages of soul love for this being who chose you to be the mother.

I suggest you do not relate this experience to your child. Instead, just be observant and notice the changes in yourself as well as the changes in your child. You can also repeat this experience again and again till you feel complete.

Welcoming a Baby's Soul into the Family

After 15 years, I closed my holistic clinic in Northwest Indiana and began traveling and teaching Radiant Heart Healing. It has been my great joy to share this unique method of spiritual healing. I met a woman named Peig who brought me to Milwaukee, Wisconsin to teach at her own holistic center. Over a period of months, I taught Peig and the healers she gathered, to use Radiant Heart Healing as well as Bringing in Radiant Babies. Several years later, Peig sent me this story.

> Charlotte, my first grandchild, is without a doubt a radiant baby! Since I'm clairvoyant, I could see her beautiful, big, bright aura the moment she was born. She is surrounded with a very bright light which gets even brighter when her parents hold her or talk to her. Our whole family is touched by having Charlotte in our lives.
>
> I have been on a spiritual path for many years and as part of my work I founded a holistic center in Milwaukee. I learned about Dr. Sharon Wesch and her work called Radiant Heart Healing, so I invited her to teach at my center. My staff and my clients benefited greatly from her Radiant Heart Healing work, and we are fortunate to have several people in the area who trained here and use her methods.
>
> Dr. Sher also introduced me to the process of Bringing in Radiant Babies. When my son Nick and his wife Holly announced they were pregnant, I taught them the process of sending spiritual love energy into the womb and sending positive thoughts to the baby. The three of us would sometimes do this together. I felt so thrilled my kids were both willing to

allow "Grandma" to bring these new ideas into the birthing process.

Charlotte was due in February, so our family Christmas gathering was just two months before her birth. We did a very special spiritual ceremony of welcoming the baby's soul into the family. Holly sat in a big chair, and we all gathered around her, placing our hands on her very pregnant belly. "All" means my bachelor brother who is in his fifties and my three sons who are 36, 34 and 30. Nick's two brothers are still single. None of them had any previous experience with spiritual work or healing, but it didn't seem to matter. They were willing to follow my lead.

I gave a little speech to start the ceremony. I wanted to keep it simple, so I just said, "Our purpose for this ceremony is to connect heart and soul to this new baby. I'm going to say the things I feel in my heart, and I invite each of you to say whatever you feel in your heart." Each of my big guys came through and said very loving things like:

> We love you, Charlotte. We welcome your soul into our family.
> This is your Great Uncle Jim. I want you to know how much I love you.

> We promise to take good care of you and protect you in this world.
> We want to connect your soul and our souls to Divine Love and wisdom. We are so grateful you chose our family.

You will always have your connection to the divine.
We are connecting our hearts and souls to your heart and
    soul.

Everyone present at this ceremony has a very special connection with Charlotte. When they hold her, she literally sinks into each of their hearts. She does not wiggle, nor does she cry. Charlotte gets more radiant around each of them. And they also get radiant when they are around Charlotte. I can actually see each of these big guys light up when they get to hold this little bundle of love. When Great Uncle Jim says hello, Charlotte always bursts out laughing. Charlotte does not seem to have this same kind of energetic reaction to people who were not at the ceremony.

I was present at the labor and delivery and was able to observe what was happening on an energetic level. At the moment of birth, a huge ball of intense white light appeared to surround Nick, Holly, and Charlotte. I could see Charlotte's big, white aura glowing within that ball of light. Holly's labor was very long and very hard—twenty-eight hours total with four hours of hard labor. During that whole time Charlotte's heartbeat stayed steady and strong, which is very unusual. As a nurse, I worked in labor and delivery for years and most babies go into distress when the mother has such a long labor. My belief is Charlotte's strong energy field allowed her to remain physically stable.

Margaret Fry, a spiritual healer from England, arrived to teach at my center several months after Charlotte's birth. Margaret has the ability to scan energy fields and communicate with babies and animals using telepathy. She did a healing session with my granddaughter with the goal of removing any birth trauma. I watched as Margaret held Charlotte to her heart and then put her down on the massage table. Then she held my grandbaby to her heart again and handed her back to me saying:

> "Charlotte told me the session is done.
> This is the first time I have seen a baby with no birth trauma."

These words from Margaret touched my heart so deeply I was moved to tears. Charlotte was able to arrive here in this world with no birth trauma. This is such a rare event! I have no statistics, but I'm sure it doesn't happen often. I know in my heart the Divine Love energy we sent into the womb all those months set the stage for this to happen. I feel blessed I followed my own "wisdom of the heart" and taught the Radiant Baby Process to Nick, Holly and my whole family. Also, I know we are blessed; Charlotte has come to bring more love and light to our family. My heart overflows with love and joy!

SPIRITUAL DISCUSSION

I was overcome with joy and gratitude when I received this story from Peig. It is my soul's mission to teach other healers to bring in the future radiant babies. Spirit guided me as I created the Radiant Baby Process with Marie and John. This story shows us others can use this gift given to me and continue the work of Bringing in Radiant Babies. As this book was going to press, I had a phone conversation with Peig. She shared she now has 6 radiant grandbabies! She also shared she has trained several other spiritual healers to teach the Radiant Baby Process. Hearing this, I felt my heart burst open and tears of joy flow down my face. I was moved to tears because I understood this spiritual process of

Bringing in Radiant Babies is spreading out to the world with no effort on my part. My dream for populating the world with radiant babies is coming true.

I invite whoever reads this story to create your own special spiritual ceremony to welcome a baby's soul into your family. If you are the grandmother of a baby coming into this world, you can follow the example presented here in Peig's story. If you are a psychotherapist or a spiritual healer, you can invite your clients to read Peig's story. Then you can show them how to create a special spiritual ceremony for a baby coming into their family.

My heart is filled with gratitude knowing this sacred work will spread and reach people I will never even meet. Heaven only knows how far it will spread and how many radiant babies will be born with a spiritual purpose of bringing more Divine Light to Planet Earth.

A Soldier Receives Healing from His Radiant Baby

I spent eight years at a large military base with my husband, Dr. Jerry Wesch, who is also a psychologist. By some miracle, the military chose him to create and direct a holistic treatment program for active duty soldiers suffering from Post-Traumatic Stress Disorder (PTSD). His clients were both men and women returning from the wars in Iraq and Afghanistan. The soldiers loved this program, and he soon had a waiting list of 200 men and women who wanted help with their PTSD. Due to nepotism policies, I could not work on the base in my husband's program. Boy, was that frustrating! However, I found a different way to be of service.

As you may know, when a soldier with PTSD returns from war, his whole family is affected by his disability. These men and women returning from war often suffer from depression, severe anxiety, nightmares, sleep issues, anger issues, and even bouts of rage. There was no program in place for the wives of these return-

ing soldiers. Some wives who were open to using spiritual healing were referred to my office looking for assistance for their own
PTSD. I loved working with these women, and they loved coming.
We shared many hours of deep healing as we worked together to
release stored emotional pain, reduce their stress levels, open their
hearts to Divine Love, and find a place of spiritual peace within the
chaos of their military lives.

Becky was one of the women who loved coming for sessions
at my office. I explained Radiant Heart Healing and she was willing to experience it. Immediately, she could feel energy moving
through her body, and she was excited to continue. She easily
learned to release the energy of negative emotions and fill her heart
with the energy of Divine Love. Gradually Becky became more
centered in herself, felt stronger each month, and felt a new connection to Spirit.

Becky had a great deal of grief about her husband. They were
married only two years when he left for Iraq. Sadly, he came back
very different. She explained to me:

> He's not the guy I married. He used to be warm and sweet
> towards me. Now that's all gone. He's depressed and angry—
> even downright mean. He just explodes if I try to talk about
> anything. He also has a TBI (traumatic brain injury) so he
> has these headaches, and he can't remember anything. I need
> help figuring out how to manage him and to get out of my
> own depression.

Becky came weekly for many months and eventually invited her husband, Charles to come for some couple's counseling. Surprisingly, he came and was also open to learning about
Radiant Heart Healing. He, too, was sensitive to energy. I checked
his chakras in one of our early sessions. His third eye was wide
open. This told me Charles was already very intuitive. Charles also

learned to open his heart and receive the energy of Divine Love. He could both see and feel Divine Light flowing into the top of his head and filling his whole chest.

Charles: I like doing this because I feel better. But I'd never tell my battle buddies. They would think all this light stuff was way out weird. Actually, I think its way out weird, but it works.

Dr. Sher: (laughing) Your secret is safe with me. I don't even know your buddies.

Eventually, I had Becky (instead of me) send Divine Love into her husband's heart. Next, I had Charles do the same for Becky. Then I showed them how to send Divine Love to each other simultaneously. They could both feel the high frequency energy of God's Love flowing into their hearts. Becky often cried tears of joy when she felt it. Charles looked like he might cry, but he stopped it. As we practiced this again and again in their couple sessions, they both shifted from being angry to feeling a hint of the love that used to exist between them. I felt such joy as I observed them sharing love once again.

One day, Charles and Becky arrived for their regular couple's session. We sat talking for a bit, and I got this intuitive idea about them having a baby. They had not mentioned anything of the sort, so I felt uneasy introducing the topic. However, that feeling just wouldn't go away.

Dr. Sher: Are you guys thinking about having a baby?

They looked at each other and both burst out laughing. Becky had sparkling eyes!

Becky: Yes! We are having a baby. We just found out a few days ago. We weren't going to tell you yet; but you guessed.

I sat there in shock for a moment. My mind started thinking of all the reasons this was the worst time for them to bring a baby into the world. First, they had almost no money. Then, Charles had all kinds of issues from his PTSD and his TBI. And Becky had her own issues of depression and doubts about the marriage relationship. Then I heard a spirit voice speaking to me. *This baby wants to come now. This courageous soul is here to bring healing to this family. This soul will be a radiant baby. You are to teach these parents to bring in a radiant baby.*

I immediately knew the arrival of this baby was divinely orchestrated. My judgements about this being the wrong time just evaporated. I could suddenly see the hidden spiritual plan involving me, Becky, Charles, and this incoming courageous soul. I understood Becky was guided to work with me a full year before getting pregnant. Along the way, she invited her husband for Radiant Heart Healing—and he came. Little did we know then their healing journey would include learning the Radiant Baby Process.

That same session I explained the Radiant Baby Process to Charles and Becky. They immediately loved the idea of bringing in a radiant baby. I was so happy we could surround this baby in Divine Light so early in the pregnancy. I knew this soul would make a smooth transition from existing on the other side in a sea of Divine Light to being surrounded with that same high frequency energy within this mother's womb. And this baby would never lose that miraculous connection to the divine. This baby would be born conscious and bring more light to this family as well as the whole planet. Each week I guided Becky and Charles to surround their baby in Divine Light.

Dr. Sher: Imagine the whole sky above the office is filled with diamond sparkling energy of Divine Light. It looks like sunlight dancing on the water. Each of you, bring that Divine Light through the roof of this building, through the ceiling and into the top of your head. Then fill your heart with this God-energy.

Becky, place your hand on your husband's heart. Send the Divine Love energy from your heart into his heart.

Charles, place your hand on your wife's heart and fill her heart with Divine Love.

Becky, send a beam of this Divine Light/Love from your heart, down your spine, into your womb. Imagine surrounding your baby in pure spiritual love. See a spark of the divine igniting Divine Light in your baby's heart. Know that as you imagine it—it really happens.

Charles, place your hands on Becky's abdomen. Send the Divine Light into your heart, down your arms, out your hands, and into her womb. Imagine your baby surrounded in Divine Light/Love. See a ball of light in your baby's heart center. Again, as you create these images in your mind, it really happens in the energy world. Now let's all send messages of love to this soul who has come to you:

We love you so much. We are sending you love energy even though we can't touch you. We talk to you every day knowing you can hear us. We look forward to holding you.

We are so happy you are here. We are sending Divine Love and our human love to your heart. You are worthy of this love. You deserve this love.

You have angels all around who are keeping you safe. We are honored you have chosen us to be your parents. We don't know if you will be a boy or a girl, but we will love you either way.

We are here to guide you on your spiritual journey here on Earth. You have come with a spiritual mission. We will support you to do your mission.

At first, I was guiding Charles and Becky to say the above messages. Then I instructed them to simply talk to their precious baby from their hearts. They began creating their own messages of love.

They both had a glow about them, and the words seemed to flow easily—coming from a higher place, I'm sure.

Becky and Charles did the Radiant Baby Process with me in the office each week. They also spent 15 to 20 minutes each day at home sending energy and messages of love to their baby in the womb. They both developed a deep love bond with this precious baby who chose them as parents. One day I said to Charles, "I think this baby is bringing healing to you." His response stunned me in the moment.

Charles: I know this baby is helping me heal. When I came home from the war, I thought of myself as a killing machine. I obsessed about that idea. It became my identity. Sending love to our baby has changed me. My heart is no longer numb. I can feel love for our baby and my wife too. That's amazing because my heart was dead for so long. I woke up one day and realized I was different. I've come to think of myself as a love machine. That's just gosh-darn amazing. Going from a killing machine to a love machine just happened without me planning it. You know, I like this new me a whole lot better.

The three of us sat in silent amazement for quite a while after this announcement from Charles. We had no words. His transformation was so profound. I silently thanked Mother Mary, my guides, my angels, and all the beings who work with me. My heart was overflowing with gratitude for the opportunity to bring another radiant baby into the world. And I was also grateful to witness the transformation of this young soldier. I heard the voice of Spirit give me a message.

> *So, behold this soldier with a radiant heart. This baby has opened her father's heart and taught him to feel love. Everything is exactly as it was meant to be.*

Weeks later Becky and Charles were blessed with the birth of a precious baby girl. As expected, all went smoothly with labor and delivery. They both felt a deep connection with their baby after all the months of surrounding her in Divine Love while she was in the womb. They brought this little bundle of joy with them when they returned for sessions. She had a big bright aura and a spark of Divine Light in her heart. She was indeed a radiant baby.

Spiritual Discussion

I wasn't surprised when I discovered Charles had a huge third eye. During my eight years at this military base, some of the active duty soldiers found their way to my practice. I discovered the same thing with every soldier—they all had a huge third eye. This was true for both men and women soldiers. Each time, I wondered why. I pondered this question for a quite a while. Then it came to me. Of course, these men and women had to use their intuition to stay alive. Day after day, they faced extreme danger, whether it was the possibility of getting blown up or shot by a sniper. I heard story after story of how their intuition kept them alive.

Working with Charles was an amazing journey. I loved watching his gradual transformation. I loved guiding him to heal his "dead heart." Of course, I knew this heart-healing couldn't fix his whole life. He still had his TBI symptoms, severe memory problems, and lots of chronic pain issues. However, he opened his heart to love again. And that was a miracle!

I've had numerous experiences where a baby came to heal somebody in the family. One was my brother. He was 60 years old and had just gone through quadruple by-pass surgery. He was depressed and had truly given up on life. He thought he had nothing to live for at this point. Then his first grandchild was born, and he came back to life. When this baby girl came home from the hospital, my brother would hold her for hours. Each time he held that baby girl, I could see his aura expand and his soul light come back into his eyes.

My brother announced to his grandbaby's mother, "I'm coming every day to take care of her. I'll be here for two hours in the mornings so you can rest, take a long bath, or do whatever you want to do." He really did follow through. Luckily, this mother liked the idea. So, for months my brother arrived every morning at 8 a.m. to hold this precious baby girl. At first glance, it looked like this grandfather was taking care of his grandbaby. Truth be told, she was taking care of him. And she healed his heart!

Bringing in Babies Who Are Spiritually Awake

Marla is an acupuncturist in Sedona, Arizona. She is also an energy healer, a spiritual medium, and a channeler. She receives profound wisdom from Spirit during her meditations, and while doing healing sessions with her clients. Marla was adopted at birth and volunteered to do a regression back into the womb to explore her prenatal experience. That regression experience is included in her adoption story (See Chapter 4 of this book). At the end of the regression, Marla received important information from Spirit about the radiant babies.

The purpose of the Radiant Baby Process is to bring babies into the world who are already spiritually awake. They will come in without a veil. They will feel one with everything on the planet. A higher consciousness will be brought in with these babies. A large group of souls has volunteered for this assignment. These babies will know what they are here to do.

The Radiant Baby Process can heal the babies of diseases while in the womb. Some may still contract to come in with dis-

abilities. This is a soul choice to learn certain soul lessons. The Radiant Baby Process will not heal babies with such a contract.

These radiant babies will come in with different frequencies than our regular people here on Planet Earth. They will carry the high, high frequencies of the Masters. These babies will be the healers and spiritual teachers of the future. They will teach their parents.

The radiant babies are being brought in to save the planet. A group of souls has volunteered to be part of saving the planet in this way. They will change our planet to be peaceful, loving and harmonious. They will bring a big transformation from where our planet is now. There is an urgency for this work to be brought forward.

Some of these radiant babies will be carrying scientific information. They will change our technology. Some of the babies will be like Tesla. They will be aware of scientific information from advanced planets. One will be born soon.

These radiant babies will receive a direct download—information flowing into their consciousness from guides, angels, and other spirit beings who also have a mission to raise the frequency on Planet Earth. The same information is available to all of us through meditation, prayer, and connection.

Spiritual Discussion

This channeled information from Marla was such a gift! Her message gave me clarity about the spiritual abilities these special babies will bring to the world. This message also gave me a much broader picture of the purpose of Bringing in Radiant Babies.

Chapter Summary

Since my experience of bringing in the first radiant baby, I have worked with numerous mothers who were doing energy healing with me before they became pregnant and stayed in my practice throughout the pregnancy. They all loved filling their hearts with Divine Light/Love and sending that high frequency energy to the developing baby in the womb. Each mother (and sometimes the father) talked to her baby, sending messages of love and encouragement to the incoming soul. Each and every baby was born with a very large, bright aura and a huge ball of Divine Light in their hearts. All of these babies (both boy and girl babies) were peaceful, calm, angelic beings. Their mothers reported receiving spontaneous compliments from strangers in restaurants and shopping malls:

> Your child is so special.
> I have never seen such a contented baby.
>
> This one is a little angel.
> Is this child always so good?
>
> I feel drawn to this baby.
> There's a special light around this child.

These babies have their hearts wide open, and their soul energy is radiating forth filling their energy field. The strangers are probably not conscious of the baby's aura being brighter or bigger, but they say things like, "I'm just drawn to this child." "This child is so special." These babies are simply wondrous examples of how human beings are naturally supposed to be— radiant and alive with soul energy flowing through the cells of their little baby bodies. I wonder what the world will be like when all babies are given the gift of bonding heart-to-heart with loving parents who have radiant hearts and are conscious of their own connection back to soul.

In our modern medicine, we have become so focused on the body and the human level of existence we have forgotten to attend to the soul. This is true in obstetrics as well as in other areas of medicine. To remedy this, I envision birthing rooms with physicians or midwives who attend to delivering the physical body of the infant and spiritual healers who attend to delivering the soul of the infant.

At this time, we have a spiritual crisis here on Planet Earth. I believe the solution to this crisis is birthing our children as radiant babies so they can live on this Earth as human beings filled with Divine Love. Then they will be consciously aware of their soul and their purpose for coming to the Earth. They will feel empowered to complete their spiritual lessons before returning to that place called eternity.

Bringing in the radiant babies is not just my work. I am only one soul who is part of a master plan involving many spirit beings coming into this world as well as numerous human beings who have volunteered to bring this work to the world. A huge number of powerful souls have volunteered to come in at this time on the planet and become the radiant babies. And a great number of soon-to-be parents have also volunteered to be the parents of these radiant babies. Nothing happens by accident. It's all meant to be. I look back at the messages from my spiritual mentor, Roy Waite. He was right all along; I am here to work with children. Little did I know back then.

These radiant babies will be born connected to their individual souls and connected to the Divine. They will never lose their connection to the Divine. They will use their high frequency energy to raise the vibrational frequency of the planet. These radiant babies will transform our world as we know it. Imagine spiritual beings with physical bodies being able to exist on Planet Earth in a state of pure light, pure love, pure physical health, and pure radiance. This is my dream for the planet, the vision I hold in my heart, and the purpose of this book.

CHAPTER TWO

HEALING PRENATAL WOUNDING

Healing prenatal wounding is a big part of my spiritual purpose. This work feeds my soul. It gives me a reason to get up every morning knowing I'm blessed to do my soul purpose one more day. Working with clients is like playing detective and searching for the soul wound that needs to be healed. I'm always so joyful when I discover prenatal wounding! That may sound strange; however, I know once the healing is complete, these searching human beings will experience a major shift in consciousness, and their life will never be the same. That is something to celebrate!

As I begin each day, I have a deep faith Spirit will be working through me, sending me inspiration and guidance to share with each dear one who comes seeking help. Furthermore, I also have complete trust in the wisdom that comes through from Spirit. At the end of the day, I bask in the Divine Love that flows through me and fills the heart of each person who has come for healing. So, each day I work with faith, trust, and Divine Love. There's nothing I'd rather be doing with my time here on Earth. Each day I thank God, Spirit, Mother Mary, the Archangel Gabriel, and all the other invisible beings who guide my life and my work. I am truly blessed.

Three Babies in One Year

Like most healers, I walked a path of healing my own issues before I ever became a psychotherapist/spiritual healer. There's an old saying, "We teach what we need to learn." So, since I'm teaching about prenatal wounding, it's rather obvious this is one of my soul lessons this lifetime. I have decided to share my experience of healing my own prenatal wounding with the hope you, the reader, will benefit from my story.

I was born into a very traditional family in Indiana. We lived on a big farm just south of Lake Michigan. It was a very stable existence with our large extended family living close by and many fun-filled family gatherings for the holidays. I was raised with midwestern values of community, hard work, and the Christian faith. My mother's claim to fame was she had three babies in one year. I've come to know that's where my emotional problems started.

Yes, three babies in one year. At first glance that sounds impossible. Yet it's true. My parents married in 1940—right before World War II. My mother told me her story like this:

I married your father, and he took me to this God-forsaken place called the farm. I was a city girl, so this was all very strange to me. We wanted to wait to have children, but I got pregnant right away with your brother. He was only four months old when I discovered I was pregnant again. Such a shock. And then I gave birth to twins! I didn't know I was having twins. So, I had these three babies in one year, and it was just too much for me. We didn't have any money, and we didn't have any help. It was just overwhelming. I've never been the same since. I had a nervous breakdown, my body fell apart, and I've been sick ever since.

I was one of the twins. We were always called "the twins," and we operated as one unit. We were energetically bonded and psychically connected with each other. My mother tells the story we both refused to eat. The doctors told my parents we had a condition called failure to thrive. Now, I know this is a baby's way of saying, "I don't want to be here. I want to go back Home." So, there's the evidence we both had a death wish right from the moment we came into this world. Imagine that!

My mother stayed a week in the hospital before going home. Because we were so tiny and underweight, the doctor thought it best we stay in the hospital for 6 more weeks. The story goes the hospital had no incubators, so one of the nurses decided to place us in the small drawers of one of the dressers. We then became known as the dresser-drawer twins. Pretty funny label, don't you think!

Twenty-five years later I birthed my first child at the same hospital. I nonchalantly mentioned I was born a twin in this same hospital and we were placed in these small dresser-drawers. The nurse gasped and said, "You're one of the dresser-drawer twins! Oh, my heavens, I took care of you for weeks after your mother went home. We had to force feed you with an eye dropper. Now here you are all grown up and having your own baby." She went down the hall telling all the nurses on the floor about the dresser-drawer twins.

Of course, my twin and I both experienced prenatal wounding, which is why we had failure to thrive. We had no idea about that at the time. I can remember as a child and even a teenager, hearing my mother tell us her story and feeling this pain in my heart every time. I felt this incredible heartache I could not even process. Why did my heart hurt? I didn't know. My mother didn't even seem upset as she repeated her story of three babies in one year. She was just repeating the facts about how our birth unfolded so close to my brother's birth. I'm sure she had no awareness of the emotional impact that story had on me or my twin. In her defense, she was a good mother who also had her own prenatal wounding. Consequently, she couldn't open her heart to any of her three babies. All of this unfolded at a very deep unconscious level as we went forward with our lives doing the best we could at the time. Now I know it unfolded according to our soul plans.

As a child I was very quiet—probably withdrawn and even depressed although I didn't know it at the time. My twin and I were both good little girls always striving to be perfect and please our parents. Our mother dressed us alike, and everywhere we went we heard, "Oh, look at the twins!" I always felt on display. We were both excellent students in school and worked hard to excel at piano lessons, baton twirling, and everything we did. I remember always feeling like I had to excel. If I wasn't perfect, I would sink into a state of depression and have almost no energy to get up in the morning. And of course, this was my own little secret. Who could I tell?

At age 27, both my death wish and my depression escalated after the birth of my second baby. I was never diagnosed, but in retrospect I know I had a severe case of postpartum depression. It was my well-kept secret. I had this new baby so I believed I should be happy. I didn't dare speak my truth and say, "I feel like I'm dying." I sometimes sat and rocked this beautiful baby girl, and realized why someone would commit suicide. I remember being at a family gathering that Thanksgiving and trying to look and act normal. Weeks later I looked at pictures taken that day, and this thought flowed into my mind. *Well, I guess I look OK.* Of course, I thought nobody guessed I was secretly falling apart.

However, Golda, my dear mother-in-law must have suspected something though she never said a word. Instead, she volunteered to help. One day she said, "I just love to be around these babies. So how about if I come over every afternoon? You and the baby can take a nap, and I will take care of my grandson." And she did. She arrived about noon, brought dinner for our family, stayed till

5 p.m. or so, and totally enjoyed taking care of all three of us. She came every day for months until she could see I was better.

We never had a conversation about my postpartum depression, but I knew she knew. She was my savior from the pain I couldn't even talk about. Looking back, I know she saved my life. We bonded forever in a deep love that had to be soul love. I often thought she must have been my mother in another lifetime. With her love she gradually drew me out of that dark time. She's on the other side now, and I know she's hearing my thoughts as I write her part of my story. I feel this deep love for her filling my heart.

Looking back, I'm horrified I rocked my precious baby and thought about suicide. Now I know my thoughts had an energy that went right into that little baby. I also recognize the energy of my thoughts and my depression surrounded that baby while she was in the womb. I was unknowingly passing on prenatal wounding to another generation. How unconscious was that? Just like my own mother, I had no awareness of what I was doing to this precious baby. The energy of forgiveness flowed out to my mother as I had that thought.

After doing this work for years, I've found prenatal wounding often runs in families. It flows down from one generation to the next without notice. Babies are born feeling unloved and starting life with a broken heart. How deeply sad. In my own family I can trace prenatal wounding through three generations—just from hearing the family stories. My mother was conceived just one year after her older brother was killed on the railroad tracks. The family story is Grandma never recovered from the death of her son. I'm sure my grandmother's womb was filled with the energy of deep grief, and my mother's baby body took that grief energy right into her little baby cells; and nobody knew.

I was 31, married with two small children, when my father died early of a heart attack at age 57. I was filled with devastating grief and my thoughts were very negative. *He's the light of my life. If my dad's not here, I don't want to be here either. I want to go be with him in the light.* Little did I know these thoughts were another sign of my own death wish. Of course, I did not tell anyone of these terrible thoughts—it was another deeply held secret. I didn't even share this with my twin or my husband. I didn't know why I was so depressed I just wanted to die. I also knew I would not take any action to kill myself because I had two little children. Who would take care of them if I left?

Finally, my grief pushed me to ask for help. A friend guided me to a wonderful grief therapist. This was the beginning of a beautiful journey of discovery called psychotherapy. Eventually that journey evolved to include spiritual healing. Forty-five years later I'm still moving forward on that same path. And I know I'll always be growing, seeking, learning, and evolving as I keep moving forward on my journey of spiritual evolution. But back to that grieving younger me.

First, I focused on healing my grief, and then I began peeling back the layers of emotional damage that I didn't even know were there. Denial is such a fascinating thing, and most people are in denial until they put themselves in a process to discover what makes them tick. Eventually, I was referred to a fascinating psychiatrist who began teaching me all about prenatal wounding. Wow! I loved working with him! Together we discovered one of my core wounds—the three babies in one-year story. We not only found it, we also healed it!

By this time on my therapy journey I knew I had been depressed most of my life. I didn't ever look depressed on the outside—no one ever suspected what was happening to me on the inside. People saw me as the All-American girl: cheerleader, baton twirler, straight A student, a leader in every way. I excelled at keeping a great public face for family and friends. I certainly did not want anyone to guess my secret. This big secret was called an agitated depression. This meant I kept myself busy, busy, busy all the time. I learned to never be still because then this heavy feeling would come over me like a cloud. I hated that feeling. It weighed me down and took all the joy out of my life. I didn't feel that oppressive weight as long as I was in constant motion focused on whatever was the next goal. Of course, I always had a new goal!

My psychiatrist explained there are three scenarios that could produce a life-long depression. First, the mother is depressed while carrying the baby in the womb. Second, the baby does not bond with the mother. Third, there is a physical separation of mother and baby within the first year. He explained how going through any one of these experiences could set the baby up to be depressed their entire life. As I listened to him, I had these thoughts. *Oh my God. I've had all three. My mother was depressed while she was pregnant with me and my twin sister. I never bonded with my mother. My twin and I were left at the hospital until we were six weeks old. No wonder I've been depressed my whole life*! It was enlightening to say the least.

This psychiatrist asked me about my thoughts and feelings when my mother would tell her story of three babies in one year. We discovered some of my early childhood decisions I had kept buried in my unconscious my whole life. I became aware I believed:

I made my mother sick. It's my fault her life was ruined (guilt for being born).

I don't want to be here. It would have been better if I had never been born (death wish).

I'm not lovable. I'll be perfect so they will love me. I will take care of others so they will love me (closed heart for receiving love).

I set my intention to heal all of this—not just make it a bit better or manage it. I wanted to eliminate it and create a whole new way to live. My healing journey included session after session of Inner-Child work, releasing the emotional pain causing my depression, and reprograming my early decisions. Eventually, I was able to shift my beliefs and transform all those early decisions. It was a long process, but eventually I achieved these shifts in consciousness:

I am lovable. I deserve love. I'm worthy of love. I love my life here on Earth. I can create a life filled with joy, peace, and love. My birth did not make my mother sick. I have no responsibility for her emotional life.

During the first 10 years of my healing journey, I used psychotherapy and stayed at the human level to heal my issues. I wasn't introduced to a spiritual view of life until years later. Now I know it's best to work at the human level and the spiritual level at the same time. Combining the two makes the healing journey move forward in a deeper, easier, and faster way.

Over time, I learned to look at my life through soul eyes and see events and relationships from a spiritual perspective. Then I began to see my experience of prenatal wounding was not an accident. My soul chose my mother knowing I would go through this experience of feeling unwanted and unloved. My soul plan was to go through this emotional pain, find a way to heal it, and then be able to lead others down the same healing path.

> I am here on Earth to experience prenatal wounding, find a way to heal it, and spread this knowledge to the world.

I Was Born Exactly as My Soul Wanted Me to Be Born

I met Sandy when I was traveling and teaching Radiant Heart Healing in Milwaukee, Wisconsin. She sent me this story about our work together.

I first met Dr. Sher three years ago on Super Bowl Sunday when she was teaching a workshop on energy healing. Attending this workshop changed my life! During that eventful day, I experienced spiritual energy firsthand. Even though the temperature outside was well below zero, the group generated such intense energy I began to sweat. This was my first experience with spiritual energy. I felt its existence even though I couldn't see it or measure it. Because I felt it, I had to shift my belief system—there really was something beyond what I could see or experience with my five ordinary human senses.

Three months later I made an appointment for an individual healing session with Dr. Sher. During our session she took me back to my birth story and led me gently back into the womb experience through a relaxation method. I was able to get in touch with deep feelings of unworthiness and realized I had carried these feelings since before I was even born.

For my mother, I was born too soon, and she was terribly ashamed of conceiving me just weeks after getting married. For my dad, I was born wrong because I was a girl rather than a boy to help him with the farm work. All of my life I needed approval from those closest to me. When I didn't receive it, I was crushed and constantly suffered with depression and anger. I also had this need to always be right in everything I did and believed, even if it meant alienating another person. I learned in my session I had to be right because being wrong as an adult would bring up my original pain of being born wrong. That pain was so intense I never wanted to feel it.

During the session, I released the deep-seated pain of feeling unlovable, unacceptable, and being born wrong. Dr. Sher guided me through a visualization to release the emotional pain stored in my cells and eliminate it from my body. I was also sobbing as I did this, and my sobbing pulled the pain from deep within. Both the visualization and the sobbing helped me to completely release the old painful emotions.

After releasing all this pain, we filled my heart with Divine Light/Love. Within seconds, I felt an inner peace I had never felt before. For days I had intense energy and a sense of euphoria about being right with God. Dr. Sher also gave me some affirmations to repeat daily to help me hold onto my shifts in consciousness. These are my new decisions: "I was born at the exact right time for me. My soul chose to be born female this lifetime, and I love being a woman. I am lovable and I deserve love just because I exist."

> Through these shifts in consciousness,
> I have been able to let go of needing the
> approval of others. What freedom!

I now know I'm lovable whether others approve or not. I now do things out of choice rather than obligation. My depression has lifted, and the anger that was always so close to the surface has been eliminated. I have become a more loving, forgiving person.

SPIRITUAL DISCUSSION

There are millions of people who believe *I was born wrong*. It can be the wrong time, the wrong sex, or the wrong circumstances for a variety of reasons. For some, it's a fleeting thought, for others, it's a pervasive thought and a deep feeling of despair that can even lead to suicide. Most people with this issue feel the need to fight to be right. It's the only way to stay above the despair and the heartache of being born wrong. The key to healing this pattern is to identify the original trauma of prenatal wounding, release the pain of that, fill the heart with Divine Light/Love, and achieve a permanent shift in consciousness. Both heartache and despair evaporate when people fill their hearts with Divine Light/Love and awaken to a new spiritual perspective. *I was born exactly the way my soul wanted me to be born. This was my soul plan so I could learn the soul lessons I came here to learn.*

I Want to Live! I've Never Said That Before.

I'll never forget working with Jim. As he came walking through the door of my office, I could see immediately he was quite sick. His aura was very close to his body and brown in color. This is never a good thing. In energy medicine, we believe the health of the physical body depends on the spiritual energy flowing through the person. Immediately, I silently asked Spirit to help me find the root cause of his depleted aura. I asked him why he was here. Jim responded:

> I heard your interview on our local radio station last week. You were talking about all these unfamiliar things like the energy of grief, heart healing, a death wish, unwanted baby issues, and love energy. I was intrigued. I never met my father, so I know I was an unwanted baby. I felt drawn to see you.

> I'm not here about my emotions. I'm looking for help for all my health issues. I'm a mess, and the doctors can't seem to help me. I have insomnia, severe digestive problems, fatigue, and constant aches and pains through my whole body. My health has deteriorated so much, I have not been able to work for almost two years.

As Jim was talking, this video started playing in my mind. Spirit gave me a vision of him as a tiny, tiny baby in the womb. My heart tuned in to his devastating heartache. It felt like a huge sword had pierced my heart. I knew without a doubt this was his pain, not mine. I also knew prenatal wounding was the root cause of Jim's physical issues although I did not share this with him. I silently thanked Spirit for giving me these clues about Jim.

I briefly explained prenatal wounding to Jim. He seemed to understand. I also explained the need to do a regression back into the womb to see what he was feeling and deciding about himself as a baby in the womb. He easily agreed. Here's a partial transcript of his regression:

Dr. Sher: What is your mother's first thought about being pregnant with you?

Jim: *Oh, Shit!*

Dr. Sher: What is she feeling about being pregnant with you?

Jim: Terrified—absolutely terrified to tell her parents!

Dr. Sher: What is your father thinking when she tells him she is pregnant?

Jim: *I can't do this. I'm leaving.*

Dr. Sher: What is he feeling?

Jim: Anger. No, it's rage!

Dr. Sher: What are you thinking about your existence there in the womb?

Jim: *I shouldn't be here. I want to go back. I don't want to be born.*

Dr. Sher: There's your death wish, loud and clear. That's why you're sick.

Jim was so quiet I wasn't sure he heard me. Then he started talking again.

Jim: I see myself in my mother's womb, and I'm sharing her fear, grief and sadness of being a pregnant, unmarried, high school teen. My father is a married man, and he abandoned her. All her feelings seem to wash over me and surround me there in the womb.

Jim said all this without a tear. I was shocked he wasn't crying. Then a very strange feeling came over my face. I felt like I was wearing some kind of mask. It was an energy mask, not a real mask. At the same time, I was gifted with a video of Jim in his second-grade classroom. I quickly decided to share this vision with Jim.

Dr. Sher: Spirit is showing me this video of you in your second-grade classroom. Your face is all stiff—like you're wearing a mask. You have the mask, so the other kids won't see your pain. You don't want them to know you have such shame about being the bastard child in this small town. Is that true?

Jim: Yes, I never wanted anyone to know how much I hurt.

Then this amazing thing happened. With my soul eyes, I saw a beam of Divine Light come through the ceiling and hit Jim right at the bridge of his nose. It looked like a bolt of lightning, but it didn't hurt. At that exact moment the energetic mask over my face cracked. It was like a windshield breaking in a million pieces. Jim's mask also broke, and he started sobbing from the very depths of his being. All the grief and heartache of being the unwanted baby came pouring out of him. For the first time in his life he cried and cried and cried. I sat next to him on a chair, quietly supporting him with my left arm around his shoulders and my right hand on his heart chakra. I was thrilled for Jim that he could experience such a release. These are the moments I wait for in my healing sessions.

Jim: I just saw myself in the womb not wanting to be born. My grief was so intense, it seemed to just burst out of my chest. I feel like somebody pulled a plug out of my heart and all this stuff flowed out of my body.

Dr. Sher: We just cleared the energy of your emotional infection from your cells. It's been there your whole life. The energy of that emotional pain has been making you physically sick. Now your body can begin to heal. We need to fill those cells with the healing energy of Divine Light/Love.

I stood behind Jim as he continued to sit on his chair. I placed my hands on the top of his head and then over his heart chakra.

He followed my lead as we visualized Divine Light flowing in from above, filling his head, then his heart, and then his whole body. This process took about 15 minutes to complete. The whole room lit up with a bright, ethereal light. It surrounded both of us. We both got extremely hot as if it were suddenly 95 degrees in this air-conditioned room. I could see Jim's aura expanding and becoming bright white with silver streaks throughout.

Jim: Wow. I'm so hot I feel like I'm in a sauna. I have my eyes closed, but I can see this light in the room. I've never seen such a bright light. It's so amazing. What is that?

Dr. Sher: That's the Light of God. It's Divine Light/Love energy. You see the Divine Light and, simultaneously, you feel the Divine Love. We imagined Divine Light flowing in from the heavens, and it did. Spirit is sending you this healing energy. Now you can get well. I want you to listen to these messages flowing through me from Spirit. Just open your mind and your heart to these words. Be the baby in the womb and take in these words from Spirit:

> *You are a beautiful child of God.*
> *You are lovable. You deserve love. You are worthy of love.*

> *Your birth unfolded exactly the way your soul planned it.*
> *There's nothing wrong with you.*

> *You deserve to live. You deserve to be here on Earth.*
> *Your soul wants you to live with peace, joy and love.*

Jim laughed with great joy and announced:

> ## I WANT TO LIVE!
> I've never said that before. I've never felt that before.
> I feel high—like I'm on drugs or something.
> I feel ecstatic, joyful, giddy.

I knew Jim had just made a re-decision. He had a spontaneous shift in consciousness. I knew he would be forever changed. We hugged goodbye, and Jim left with his big, bright shiny aura. I took a moment and thanked all the spirit beings who assisted with this healing session. The video that came from Spirit gave me the key to finding Jim's death wish. He called three weeks later, and I held my breath as I listened. I didn't know what he would say.

> I called to thank you for that session. Afterwards, many of my physical problems just went away. I started sleeping immediately the first night, and my digestion problems cleared up within the next two weeks. My severe fatigue went away, and 50% of my body aches and pains cleared up. I feel almost normal again. I went to see my acupuncturist who is clairvoyant. He couldn't believe my new, big beautiful aura. He told me my energy field was totally transformed. He asked me what happened, and I said, "I really don't know. I sat with this lady from Indiana who works with energy. We did this release, and then this bright light filled me and the whole room. She said it was Divine Love." He smiled and said, "Yes, that would do it."

Jim returned for a healing session every month for the next year when I was traveling and teaching in Florida. He was so drawn to the work he decided to get certified in Radiant Heart Healing. He attended my weekend workshops to learn to be a healer. Jim was a dedicated student and a joy to have in the training group. I watched him transform over the next year from a left brained accountant to a right brained intuitive healer. It was my absolute joy to be the catalyst for his transformation. Jim wrote me this letter at the end of his training:

> Thank you, Dr. Sher, for inspiring me to create a whole new life for myself. I've realized in our very first session I made a decision to affirm life. I will never forget shouting, "I want to live!" It just came bursting out of me. I believe that re-decision truly opened me up to experience love at a deeper level. This new feeling seemed to spread to people around me—like my wife and my 4-year-old son. I draw on the light whenever I need it. I also believe that decision to affirm life had an immediate effect on my physical health. Over the next six months I got better each month. I'm deeply grateful to have my health back.
>
> I now view that session as the major starting point on my path of emotional and spiritual growth. It was the catalyst that set everything in motion. Three years later I am still evolving to higher levels, and I am not at all the same person who walked into your office years ago. I love being a healer. I have become very intuitive, and I am able to communicate with beings in the Spirit World. My life is so much richer! I now live in an expanded state of consciousness.

SPIRITUAL DISCUSSION

I still have that letter. I keep it as a reminder of the importance of healing prenatal wounding. Jim's story is a great example of a baby creating a death wish in the womb. It often lies there dormant for years and at some later time kicks in, triggering a life-threatening illness. Healing Jim's death wish was the catalyst for his physical body to begin healing. When anyone is sick, I begin by looking for their conscious or unconscious death wish. Most often, it started in the womb. However, a person can form a death wish later in life when a loved one dies, or some other emotional trauma happens in their life.

When I had my holistic medical center, I worked with many cancer patients. While the doctors worked with their physical body, I focused on finding and healing their death wish. Some cancer patients were conscious of their death wish; however, they had no clue that wishing to die could affect their physical health. Most were totally unaware of a death wish so I spent a lot of time educating my cancer clients about this possibility. My goal always was to help each person create a strong will to live.

Shouting with Joy, I Want to Live!

Denise came to me with the goal of healing her life-long anxiety. At the time of our session she was 57 years old and working as an intensive care nurse. The anxiety she had her whole life had recently escalated to debilitating panic attacks. She was thinking she would have to resign as a nurse because she feared her panic attacks could get her so off balance, she might make a mistake and cause a patient to die. Denise was blaming her panic attacks on menopause, but intuitively, I knew differently. My intuition said it had to be an unresolved emotional issue. Before she arrived, I asked Spirit for the root cause of her panic attacks. I heard a voice within my head say, *prenatal wounding*. I began the session with the intention of discovering the root cause of her emotional pain.

Denise began by talking about her current life, her anxiety and her hormones. Intuitively, I knew this anxiety problem was not about her hormones. I gently shifted her focus.

Dr. Sher: Let's talk about your childhood. What do you know about your birth story?

Denise: I know I was a change of life baby. My presence was a great distress to both my parents.

There was the confirmation I was looking for! So, I explained about prenatal wounding and that being the surprise baby could be the root cause of her life-long anxiety. Of course, she had never heard of prenatal wounding, but she seemed to trust me and was willing to explore her prenatal experience.

First, I checked her chakras with my pendulum. The energy patterns of her chakras told me some interesting information. Her root chakra, the one at the base of her spine, was totally closed. There was no spiritual energy flowing through this chakra. Whenever I see this, I know the client has a death wish. This is a desire, sometimes conscious, sometimes unconscious to leave this planet and go to the light on the other side. Denise shared she felt suicidal for many years; however, she also knew she would never take her own life. She never understood where her suicidal ideas were coming from; but she was aware of these ideas since she could remember.

I gently suggested her death wish was formed in the womb before she was ever born. She looked at me with a shocked look on her face. Actually, she was quite speechless in the moment. Denise's heart chakra was also closed. As a nurse I knew she must have great compassion for her patients. I suggested her heart was too open to giving and closed to receiving. She felt this was correct.

Denise: I've never felt loved or lovable. I've never shared that with anyone.

Dr. Sher: This belief can also be caused by prenatal wounding.

I continued checking her chakras. Her intuition chakra was wide open and spinning clockwise with amazing speed.

Dr. Sher: I'll bet you are highly intuitive.

Denise: Yes, I've been seeing and interacting with spirits my whole life. They seem like real people to me. At age three, I could see my spirit grandmother, and all my aunts and uncles on the other side. This scared my parents so I learned to stop talking about all the spirit relatives I could see.

Knowing Denise was so spiritually awake, I knew we would have a profound healing session. I explained I wanted to regress her back into the womb and then ask some questions. All she needed to do was answer my questions off the top of her head—that means using her intuition, not her logical mind. She followed my lead and easily became the little baby in the womb. While in this state, I asked her five questions and recorded her answers.

Dr. Sher: Go to the moment your mother first discovers she is pregnant with you. What are her thoughts?

Denise: She has all negative thoughts. *I don't know what I'm going to do. I'm so tired. My other kids are almost raised. What if this change of life baby is not normal? What if this baby is deformed or mongoloid?*

Dr. Sher: What is your mother feeling?

Denise: She's filled with anxiety. She has so much fear she can't sleep. Her whole being is filled with fear. She is crying and depressed about having this baby.

Dr. Sher: Imagine your mother telling your father, "We are pregnant. We are going to have another baby." What are his thoughts?

Denise: He's an alcoholic and a spender. He immediately gets drunk. *What are we going to do with another child? We can't afford this baby. We have no money for this.*

Dr. Sher: What is Dad feeling emotionally?

Denise: He's frustrated. No, he's really, really angry. He's spewing anger everywhere. He's angry I exist.

Dr. Sher: Now be yourself. Be the little baby in the womb. What are you deciding about yourself?

Denise: *I don't want to come out! I will be a disappointment when I'm born. I can never live up to their expectations. Are they going to want me when I come out? I don't want to be born.*

Dr. Sher: There's your death wish. And what are you feeling in the womb?

Denise: I'm terrified.

Dr. Sher: You took on your mother's anxiety in the womb. What else are you feeling?

Denise: My heart hurts. My heart hurts so much I can't stand it.

Denise began sobbing uncontrollably at this point. I guided her to release this pain by giving it a color and visualizing it leaving her body. She was having trouble doing this, so I switched to toning. I guided Denise to take a deep breath and make a long tone—as loud and long as she could hold it. She loved doing this and felt immediate relief of her heartache. This toning allowed her to release rather quickly. Suddenly, as the release finished, she shouted with joy, "I want to live!" She actually stood up and yelled it out. Then she started laughing and laughing and laughing.

This was such an emotional moment. We were both crying tears of absolute joy! Again, these are the healing moments I wait for in my sessions. At this moment, she had a huge spontaneous shift in consciousness. Denise went from *I just want to die* to *I want to live*. Her death wish was healed. I knew this at the very core of my being. She would never have suicidal thoughts again.

I still wanted to help Denise with her belief *I'm not lovable*. So, we did a Healing Back in Time. Denise chose her birth mother to be her mother in this healing. We created a scene with Denise as a baby in her mother's womb, but this time it was filled with Divine Light/Love.

I was the voice of Denise's mother giving her all the loving messages a baby needs to hear:

> We're so happy you're here.
> We're so glad you chose our family.
> We love you and we'll support you
> on your earthly soul journey.

Denise absorbed all these beautiful love messages. She literally sucked the light into her heart. Her heart became radiant, and her aura filled with this incredible bright light. There was no question she felt the energy of Divine Light/Love.

Then suddenly the spirit of Denise's mother appeared in front of us. She looked young, like in the prime of her life. Denise could see her face clearly and received these messages from her. *I'm so sorry I rejected you in the womb. I had no idea I was hurting you. Please forgive me and open you heart to all the love I'm sending you now from the other side. My love for you can never be broken. It is a forever love. I'm always around. Look for me and feel my love.*

Obviously, Denise's mother was present and observing our healing session the whole time. There was nothing more I needed to say. We simply sat together enjoying the sacred space and absorbing the energy of Divine Light/Love in the room. This healing session was complete.

Spiritual Discussion

While in the womb Denise took on the energy of her mother's anxiety. I've seen this time and time again. Every emotion has an energy. The energy of the mother's anxiety flows down through her body, into the womb, and fills the cells of the little baby. Then the baby carries this energy of the mother's anxiety into adulthood. All of this is happening on an unconscious level so it's nearly impossible for the person to know how to heal this anxiety that was imprinted in the womb.

Notice how the discomfort of her anxiety pushed Denise to search for some kind of relief. In her searching, Spirit guided her to my office so she could heal her prenatal wounding. It was no accident we were brought together. It was all part of her soul plan to experience prenatal wounding and then somehow find a way to heal it. In the process, Denise also had a spiritual awakening. She awakened to a life-changing connection to the light during the Healing Back in Time. That is exactly what her soul wanted her to do. My heart is filled with gratitude that Spirit brought us together and guided this healing session. I'm also grateful to Denise that she allowed me to guide her through this regression. That took a lot of trust.

Spirits often spontaneously appear in my Radiant Heart Healing sessions. It happens even with first-time clients. Sometimes it's a spirit loved one, sometimes angels, sometimes Mother Mary. I never know who will show up. The way I work, the clients receive the visions while I hold sacred space. This means I'm quiet and sending Divine Light/Love into the clients' heart. The Divine Light/Love raises the clients' frequency so they are able to connect with the Spirit World. Then Spirit sends the perfect visions or messages for the miracle of healing to occur. My goal always is to turn the session over to the wisdom of Spirit and trust the clients will receive exactly what they need.

I did a phone interview with Denise 18 months after our session. Denise gave me this report:

My life is so much improved in the last year and half. My anxiety is 75% reduced since my prenatal session, and I was able to go off my anxiety medications. I'm so happy about that. Before our session I had disconnected from the light. Also, I could not see an end to my human struggle. Since clearing my death wish, I no longer have suicidal thoughts, and I'm so excited about living my life. My re-decision to live has motivated me to take much better care of myself. Now I do yoga, eat a plant-based diet, keep my thoughts positive, spend time focused on the beauty of nature all around me, and put a bubble of light around me when I go to work at the hospital.

All of this keeps me balanced and joyful. This may sound strange, but I've developed a closer relationship with both my spirit mother and my spirit father who are alive and well on the other side. They come to me more often and we share so much love. I'm thrilled I have this natural gift of connecting with the Spirit World. This allows me to feel all the love flowing from my spirit relatives on the other side.

I Feel Worthy of Shining My Light out to the World

Kerry came for a Radiant Heart Healing Session looking for assistance with her life-long anxiety. Of course, I was reminded of Denise's experience presented in the previous story. When Kerry first came to me, she was 40 years old. She reported feeling overwhelmed with anxiety her whole life. She told me she had pushed herself to graduate from college with a master's degree in counseling and was working as a mental health counselor in a clinic. She was filled with anxiety during school and while functioning as a professional counselor. She somehow learned to override this terrible feeling, but it never went away.

Kerry intuitively knew her anxiety had something to do with feeling emotionally rejected by her mother all her life. Kerry lived with her mother's constant criticism and made an early childhood decision. *Something must be wrong with me.* Kerry was raped at age 20 and became pregnant from this experience. Of course, this increased her anxiety immensely. She decided to get an abortion and was at the abortion clinic when the technician made a minor mistake. She accidently moved the ultrasound screen and Kerry caught a glimpse of her baby in the womb.

Kerry: My baby looked like a little lima bean. After seeing this I ripped off all the attached medical equipment and walked out the door. I just could not end my baby's life. To me, this seemed like a divine intervention. God wanted me to keep this baby. From that moment forward, I started calling my baby Bean. He's now 20 years old and six feet tall, but I still call him Bean to this day. He's fine with that, but he does say, "Don't let anyone hear you call me that."

Kerry took this baby into her heart and loved him deeply. She never told him that she was raped and she never mentioned his father. Somehow, she was able to accept this child into her heart and give him everything she wanted but didn't get from her own mother. We continued to talk about Kerry's life.

Kerry: I have a very kind, loving husband who adores me. Strangely, I don't feel worthy of him. I don't know where this feeling comes from, but I can't seem to shake it.

When I heard that comment, I intuitively knew Kerry had prenatal wounding. In the first few minutes she mentioned two classic symptoms of the unwanted, unloved baby. The first was, "*Something is wrong with me.*" The second was, "*I'm unworthy of love.*"

So, I decided to explore Kerry's birth story. I wanted to know about the pregnancy, not about labor and delivery. I asked Kerry if her parents were married when she was conceived. Kerry shared that her mother was seven months pregnant when she walked down the aisle. Bingo!

That's all I needed to confirm my suspicion Kerry had prenatal wounding. I explained the theory of prenatal wounding and suggested to Kerry her birth story was the original trauma and the root cause of her lifelong anxiety. She had never heard of prenatal wounding, yet she believed me and trusted me to do a gentle regression back into her mother's womb. I gently led her back to that early time after conception. Once she was there, I asked her to recall her mother's thoughts and feelings, her father's thoughts and feelings, and the decisions she made about herself.

I explained her spirit was there the whole time and would be able to answer these questions. Her spirit knew everything her mom and dad were thinking and feeling when they discovered her existence. Her spirit also knew everything Kerry decided about herself in the womb at that time. These decisions were made by Kerry's spirit even before she had a brain.

Dr. Sher: What were your mother's first thoughts when she discovered she was pregnant with you?

Kerry: *Oh, shit! Now what the fuck am I going to do? How can I tell my mother? How can I tell the father? I don't want this baby. I want to live my dream of joining the military. I don't want to give up cigarettes.*

Dr. Sher: What is she feeling?

Kerry: She's scared. She is very, very anxious. She is overcome with anxiety. She can't sleep. She's so sad she has to give up the life she planned. Also, she's pissed.

Dr. Sher: Imagine your mother telling your father "I'm pregnant. We're going to have a baby." What are his first words?

Kerry: I love you. Let's get married. We can figure this out.

Dr. Sher: What is your father feeling?

Kerry: He's excited I'm here. He loves me. I am his first child. He's somewhat nervous because he doesn't know how to raise kids.

Dr. Sher: What are you feeling as you hear their thoughts and feelings?

Kerry: I'm terrified to be born. Oh, my goodness. I'm filled with anxiety while I'm a baby in the womb!

Dr. Sher: Yes. You have your mother's anxiety in your little baby cells. You are still carrying that energy as an adult. Let's give it a color and imagine releasing it to the Universe. It wasn't yours to begin with.

Kerry: It's lime green and I see it flowing out. Wow! That's a relief. I like this lighter feeling.

Dr. Sher: What are you deciding about yourself as the baby in the womb?

Kerry: *I'm not wanted. I'm an inconvenience. I'm a burden. I'm sorry I exist. Something must be wrong with me. I'll never be good enough. I'm not worthy of love. I'm a fighter. I have to keep fighting to live.*

As Kerry expressed these beliefs about herself, she began to feel a deep ache in her heart. She kept pressing her hand against the pain in her chest. Tears flowed down her face releasing a deep sadness that had been there from her early days in the womb. She became aware of the devastating grief she'd been holding in her heart since she was only a little group of cells. I intervened to assist her releasing this deep grief.

Dr. Sher: Ask Spirit to give you a color to represent your emotional pain.

Kerry: Red.

Dr. Sher: Now imagine that red grief energy is in every cell of your upper torso. Give every cell permission to release the red. See the red energy running in little rivers out of your cells and collecting in your chest cavity.

Kerry: I see that happening. I have a huge ball of red energy in my chest. It looks like a big sun.

Dr. Sher: Now imagine that ball turns into a balloon. Visualize the balloon opening and a geyser of red energy spewing forth from your chest.

Kerry: OK, I see that. It's huge and has a lot of force. The red geyser is just bursting out of my chest. Now it seems to be slowing down. Now there's just a little puddle of red in my chest.

Dr. Sher: We have to remove it all. What can you do to release this last bit of red in the puddle?

Kerry was quiet for a time. Then she exclaimed:

Oh, my God! A huge angel wing just came over my left shoulder. This wing is touching the red puddle. It's soaking up all the red energy. Now the whole wing is red, and the puddle is empty. This is just amazing! This angel came to help me.

Dr. Sher: Spirit just created a miracle for you. Notice, I did not mention anything about an angel coming to assist. This beautiful angel wing came as a gift from Spirit. You deserve this gift of healing.

Now we need to do a Healing Back in Time. I want you to choose a new mother and we are going to give you an experience of being loved by this mother while in the womb. As we do this in your imagination, your wounded inner child will experience it as real.

Kerry: I choose my husband's Aunt Chris. Everyone calls her Mama Chris. She's always a loving mother to whoever needs love. She has loved me from the time I joined his family.

Dr. Sher: Imagine Mama Chris sitting in a rocking chair. She is so full of joy because she has just discovered she is pregnant with you. She's talking to you, and you can feel the energy of her thoughts and her feelings. Mama Chris knows how to connect to the Divine Light/Love, fill her heart with this love, and send it into her womb. You are a tiny group of cells swimming in this Divine Light/Love energy. You were a soul swimming in the Divine Light/Love of Heaven before you chose to come to Earth. Now you have this Divine Light/Love surrounding you while you exist in Mama Chris's womb. You feel right at home. You can be a baby in the womb and still keep your connection to the Divine.

Mama Chris is talking to you and giving you the messages every baby needs to hear. I will be her voice speaking to you:

I love you with all my heart and soul. I'm so happy you chose me as your mother. I am here to assist you on your soul journey.

Your soul has chosen to be a girl or a boy. I don't know which you will be, but I know I will love you whatever you choose to be.

Your soul has also chosen a mission or purpose for your life here on Earth.

I don't know what this is, but I promise I will help you find your purpose and help you accomplish whatever that may be.

You are precious. You deserve to be here with me.

You are a beautiful Child of God. You are loved just because you exist.

You deserve all my love. You are enough. You are a joy to my heart.

You can flow through life with ease. You have many angels to assist you with your life purpose.

I can't wait until I can hold you and see you and touch you. I promise to love you forever.

Your heart is glowing with Divine Love. Right now, you are a radiant baby filled with light and love.

Enjoy the experience of feeling your heart filled with spiritual love. This is what you deserve in life.

Kerry: I'm crying because I feel so loved. I've never felt this kind of energy in my heart. It's so uplifting. My whole chest feels full and expanded. I also feel this wonderful warmth in my chest. I'm bursting with love.

As we finished the session Kerry looked entirely different. She was smiling and glowing, and her anxiety simply vanished. She described feeling a sense of deep spiritual peace in her heart. She felt all this for the first time in her life! Next, I suggested Kerry do this practice daily after returning home:

See yourself sitting in a quiet place listening to soft music. Imagine the sky above you is filled with the sparkling diamond light like when the sun shines on the water. This is the energy of Divine Light/Love. You can bring it into your heart every morning. Visualize a water fall of this Divine Light/ Love flowing into the top of your head and filling every cell in your head.

Then imagine a beam of this light flowing down into your heart. Fill your heart with this Divine Light/Love. Hold both hands over your heart and hold this ball of light with your hands while repeating these love affirmations:

I am a Child of God, and I know God loves me.

I also know my soul loves me.

I'm willing to open my heart and receive all this spiritual love.

I am worthy of this love.

I deserve this love.

I know I'm lovable.

SPIRITUAL DISCUSSION

I've worked with other women who conceived a baby after being raped. These previous cases did not have a good outcome. One mother displaced her anger for the rapist onto her daughter. This child grew up hearing this vicious verbal abuse: "I tried to abort you. I hate you. You look like my rapist. I wish you had died. I can never forget that rapist, because every time I look at you, I'm reminded of him." When this child became an adult, she attempted suicide numerous times before seeking treatment. It took a long time for her to heal the death wish instilled by her mother's abusive messages.

Kerry is a very strong woman with a profound mother love. She opened her heart to her baby even though he was the product of her rape. She took him into her heart and filled her baby with the energy of mother love and Divine Love from her soul. All this love energy protected him from developing even a hint of prenatal wounding. This was truly a miracle!

The deepest healing moment for Kerry was during the Healing Back in Time. The love energy that flowed from her new mother affected Kerry in a very deep way. When Kerry felt the love energy in her heart, she became a radiant being filled with light and love. Again, we see: Love is the most powerful healing force on the planet.

Kerry gave me this feedback several months after her session:

My healing session was a life changer. I stopped yearning for attention and love from my mother. This is a big change. I used to be on the phone with Mom, telling her events in my life hoping to get noticed. She had nothing to give. I would hang up and feel bad for days. Now that I'm feeling loved inside, I can accept that's just how she is. When my husband says, "You look so nice today." I just take it in and feel good. I feel worthy of his compliments. I used to have my guard up when he gave me a compliment. I've spent most of my life keeping myself back in the shadows. Now I believe my existence is not a burden; I'm just as important as other people. Now, I feel worthy of shining my light out to the world. I love this new me!

A PTSD Veteran with Angel Wings

James is a highly sensitive guy with a really big heart. He is 6 feet 5, very lanky, and covered with tattoos. At first glance he looks like a biker dude, but when you get to know him, he's just one big teddy bear. He's so tall he has to bend way down, and I have to go on my tip toes to share a hug. It's worth the stretch because this guy gives great hugs!

The best thing that ever happened to James is he met and married his soul mate. These two share a deep soul love that is palpable when you're in the same room with them. The worst thing that ever happened to James is getting a diagnosis of a neurological condition similar to Multiple Sclerosis, but much worse. He lives in constant nerve pain and has difficulty walking. The prognosis is not good. James is coping quite well with his physical illness because he has two pillars of strength: the soul love from his wife, and a deep faith in God.

James is a veteran and suffers from PTSD after repeated violent incidents that occurred while he was in the military. My husband, Dr. Jerry Wesch, was treating him for PTSD and road rage. Dr. Jerry suspected prenatal wounding, so he referred James to me.

James was nervous but also excited at the beginning of our healing session. He came because he trusted Dr. Jerry so much. He simply transferred that trust to me. I also had a bit of trepidation. Would this military veteran be able to let go enough to regress back into the womb? Would he be able to sense spiritual energy? I had no idea. As always, I trusted Spirit would be working with the two of us to create the perfect healing experience for him.

James's Prenatal Regression

I was amazed James relaxed so easily and followed my lead to regress and become the baby in his mother's womb. Imagine this big military guy lying on my healing table, sharing his thoughts and feelings as he became the baby in the womb. It was such a delicate, precious moment. Here's his description of his experience:

> I'm in the womb. It's pitch black, and I feel alone. Mom is happy to be pregnant, and she wants a boy. I can hear my parents having a disagreement. They are disagreeing about me. Dad is angry because Mom is pregnant. He's very scared about money. I feel safe in the womb even though I'm alone and not cared for. I want to be born.

> I'm out in the world, and I feel set aside. I see myself as a tiny baby, only a week old. My mother is breast feeding me, but she seems annoyed in some way. I have these huge eyes looking up at her. I look up at her, and there's nothing there—just nothing. I feel this soul aching heartache. I'm just little, teeny tiny. How can she not love a little baby? How could she not love me? I can't understand how a mother could not love her newborn baby.

James was sobbing as he felt the deep pain of not bonding with his mother. He let himself go into deep wracking sobs that shook his whole body. He had hot tears running down his face for a very long time. I kept my hand on his heart while letting his feelings flow until they were spent. As the deep emotional release finished, he was very quiet lying on his back on my healing table. I honored his need for quiet before moving forward.

Dr. Sher: Let's do a Healing Back in Time. I want you to pick another mother so you can experience being in a womb filled with Divine Light/Love. It could be an aunt, a grandmother, or a spiritual mother like Mother Mary or Quan Yin.

James: I have a strong connection with Mother Mary.

Dr. Sher: So, imagine you are in Mother Mary's womb, and it's filled with all this Divine Light/Love. Just let yourself be in the light. Soak it up. You deserve this love.

I could feel James going deep within himself—he was in a gentle hypnotic trance. I hardly spoke for a full 30 minutes while I sent healing energy into his heart. My intention was to stay out of the way and hold sacred space for him to go wherever Spirit wanted to take him. During this time, James described some of what he was seeing in the Spirit World. He kept switching between laughter that shook his whole body and weeping with incredible joy. With his few words, his laughter, and his hot tears I could tell he was having an amazing journey into the light. He later gave me this full description of his journey:

> I was in Mother Mary's womb. There was this grey veil with Divine Light behind it. At first, I just got glimpses of the light. Then the veil lifted, and I was surrounded with this amazing bright light. It was not blinding. It was the brightest, most beautiful light I've ever seen in my life. There are just no words.
>
> Then I found myself outside Mary's womb but still in this beautiful light. I was pure soul flying without my body. I came up above the earth. I saw the entire expanse of the Universe.

Awesome is the only word. It was pure love. I felt a part of everything. I was in everything and everywhere at the same time. I was omnipresent. Infinite does not begin to explain the depth of what I was experiencing.

I saw my wife and felt like we were a part of each other. There was so much soul love between us. I saw my grandfather who was the only person who loved me as a child. I felt this incredible love for him and from him. We became one with each other. Then I was out in the Universe again. I was part of the light. I was part of everything. I never felt so much joy or so much love. Words cannot do it justice. I felt so much of all the beautiful things in life. It was awesome. I was in pure awe of this vast, immense, infinite Universe.

Then I was aware of having a body. I reached behind me and touched angel wings. I actually felt the feathers on my wings. The wings were attached to my back. I felt pure joy and elation like I've never experienced before. Then I flew past a whole bevy of angels. They were sounding trumpets and singing. It was the most incredible thing. I felt my whole being filled with awe. Again, there are no words to adequately describe the beauty of my experience.

> I felt like I touched God.
> It was so beautiful I wept with pure joy.

At one point I saw a beautiful little blue bird. He was singing this incredibly beautiful song. I felt myself become part of the melody. I was one with the notes of his song. It was pure tranquility. I was overwhelmed with pure joy once again. Hot tears continued to flow down my face.

I've been ill for 10 years now with a neurological condition that keeps getting progressively worse and causes constant extreme physical pain. While I was in the light, my body pain was just gone. I think being in that high vibrational energy lifted me above my physical body. That was so amazing! I almost couldn't believe I was without pain.

I felt my soul come back into my body on Dr. Sher's healing table. I was pulled back in because I had this terrible need to pee! (Laughing.) I opened my eyes and everything in the room was more vibrant. My body was vibrating with energy. I was full of joy. I couldn't stop crying. I felt free. I felt so special. I just laid there and cried tears of joy and love for a long time. I felt such deep peace. Dr. Sher told me I was out of my body for maybe 30 minutes. It felt timeless to me. If everyone was able to experience this, it would change the world.

James's Report One Week Later

I'm so different. I feel lighter. I have no resentments towards anyone—all my anger and angst are gone somehow. I'm filled with forgiveness towards everyone who did me wrong throughout my life—including my parents and my worst enemies.

Sometimes I feel like I'm not fully back here on Earth. I lose time, and I feel raw. My whole being still feels filled with the light. I cry on a dime. I'm not sad. I'm crying because I feel so loved. When I was in first and second grade, I had this pervasive thought there was something wrong with me. That's just gone. I feel whole now. I wake up happy. I feel worthy of love for the first time in my life. That's huge for me.

I used to have a very short fuse. I would blow up without even knowing it was coming. Now I feel in control. There's nothing that can light my fuse. I used to have this terrible problem with road rage. I would be overcome with this white rage if I thought another driver was doing something stupid. Now I just laugh at the crazy drivers and even feel lots of compassion for them. This all feels very strange—like I'm a totally different person.

I was raised Catholic, so I was taught to fear God. I spent my whole life being afraid I was going to hell. Now after being in the light, my fears are gone. I experienced God's Divine Love, and I'm transformed. I know there is no evil.

A miracle happened when I returned home. My wife was recovering from a spinal surgery and had been in excruciating pain for weeks. Somehow my high vibration influenced her, and she had the best three days of her recovery. Her pain went way down. I was not doing any healing with her—just being in my energy field raised her above the pain she had been experiencing. We were both amazed and so grateful.

Spiritual Discussion

Needless to say, I was amazed by this experience with James. And to think I doubted this military guy could even do a regression! I felt a deep sense of gratitude that Spirit assisted us so we could create such a mystical experience. I remember six other times over 40 years when a client had a similar extended experience of the light.

I know James, like all the others, experienced a transformation at the core of his being.

James's spiritual experience is very much like a near death experience (NDE), except he didn't have to die, cross over, and come back to tell the world about the light. Millions of people who have had a NDE report the exact same details that James described: the beauty of the light, immense love, oneness with everything, profound joy, release of all negative feelings, and an experience of touching God.

Transcendence is the spiritual/psychological term used to categorize James's peak experience. Transcendence refers to the very highest level of human consciousness. In this mystical state people experience exactly what James reported. I believe every person on Earth is capable of having a transcendent experience. Opening yourself to such an experience usually involves combining intention with dedication to some spiritual practice such as meditation, yoga, or sessions with a spiritual healer.

We did a second session with the goal of James having another sacred journey into the light. There was no need to repeat the prenatal regression. Amazingly, he immediately went into the light and found himself once again flying through the Universe as a soul without a body. We continued with these sessions every other week for a few months. Each time James reported being in the light and interacting with various spirit beings. And each time his physical pain was greatly reduced for days after these sessions.

I suggested to James he could evolve to the point of being able to transcend into the light at home without my assistance. At first, he believed that to be impossible, but I encouraged him to hold that intention as a goal for the future. I'm thrilled to report James actually accomplished this goal about four months after his first transcendence experience. He is now able to put himself in a meditative state, leave his body, and find himself flying out into the light. And, each time, his debilitating physical pain is greatly reduced. James considers each healing journey a gift from God, Mother Mary, the angels and all his spirit guides.

Our Future Generations Will All Be Radiant Babies

Survivor is the best word I know to describe this wonderful client, colleague and friend, Luann. She started as a client about a year ago; now our relationship has evolved into much more.

This remarkable 65-year-old woman has shown great determination to overcome the numerous traumas in her life. She has healed from a lifetime of vicious physical, mental, and emotional abuse from a mentally ill mother. At age 37 she was in a car accident that left her in chronic pain and destroyed her career. At age 60, she had an attack of the H1N1 flu that caused her to have a near death experience and then be in a coma for six weeks. All this left her brain damaged so badly, it took five years of rehabilitation for her to heal her brain and resume a normal life once again. This woman healed all these tragedies because she just never gave up. She kept believing she could heal, worked hard every day, and prayed for miracles. Her prayers were answered!

At first glance, Luann seems like an ordinary woman who is a wife, mother, grandmother, career woman, and dear friend to many. When you dig deeper, you find she is also a Reiki Master Teacher who taught healing classes in New York for 30 years. She has hundreds of Reiki students all over the United States. In spite of all her traumas, or maybe because of all her traumas, Luann has evolved into a powerful spiritual healer who brings special blessings and healing to many who are suffering.

Luann has had psychic abilities since childhood. At age seven, she could see a big white angel in her room every night. She has honed her spiritual gifts by training in many different spiritual healing modalities. Consequently, she is a highly sensitive person who lives at a very high vibration. She is frequently gifted with visions of Mother Mary, Jesus, numerous 12-foot golden Hathor angels, and Magdalana, her spiritual mentor, who now communicates from the other side. These spiritual beings send her messages including loving guidance about her life. As you read her story, you will see she is a remarkable person with extraordinary spiritual gifts.

One day in our two-hour weekly session, I felt guided to explain the concept of prenatal wounding to Luann. Of course, she had no awareness this could be the root cause of some of her life-long emotional pain. Then I invited her to do the work to heal this emotional wound. She trusted me, so I was able to do gentle hypnosis and regress her back to the womb. From that position we could explore the messages she received from her parents and the decisions she made about herself in the womb. Here's a partial transcript of that session:

Dr. Sher: Your mother became pregnant just a few months after she miscarried her first baby. What were your mother's first thoughts when she discovered she was pregnant with you?

Luann: *I'm trapped. I have no place to run. Where can I go? I don't want this baby.*

Dr. Sher: What is Mom feeling?

Luann: She's scared. Actually, it's overwhelming fear. There is no joy.

Dr. Sher: What is your father thinking?

Luann: *This is good. Another baby. Now my wife can forget about the other one.*

Dr. Sher: What is he feeling?

Luann: He's happy I'm here. He's not exuberant, just happy. He's also terrified. *What if she loses another baby? What will she be like?*

Dr. Sher: Now be yourself. Be the baby in the womb. What are you experiencing?

Luann gave me this description of her experience in the womb:

I'm so hot. She's taking a hot bath. She's trying to get rid of me in the hot. She's done this more than once. I always outsmart her. I curl myself into a ball and roll up under her ribs. It's still hot, but it's not unbearable. I'm feeling worn out. It is such hard work to save myself. She tried to 'hot me out.' I know she is trying to abort me, but I won't go.

I can hear my mother's thoughts and feel the energy of those thoughts. She's worrying. These repetitious thoughts go around and around in her head. I don't like this. It disturbs me. It's all worry thoughts. Regular people don't have thoughts like these.

I'm fighting for survival against these thoughts!

My husband doesn't love me. I don't like my husband. I don't like this baby. I'm disgusted at my body changes. I feel deformed, misshapen, gangly. I'm embarrassed to be pregnant. It's proof I've had sex with my husband. I wanted to be chaste like the nuns. I hate my husband for getting me pregnant. I hate this baby of his. I was going to leave him after my other baby died, but then I found myself pregnant again.

I realize my mother has a mental illness. These are not just bad thoughts. These are pervasive negative thoughts that keep her brain agitated. She has no control over this. She can't seem to stop it. She just gets worse and worse each month.

With those words, Luann dissolved into sobs releasing her deep heartache about being the unwanted, unloved baby in the womb. She also released her deep pain of knowing her mother tried to abort her while a baby in the womb. She wept from the very depths of her being. I held her like a little child as she cried buckets of hot tears. We continued for a very long time until she was all cried out.

Luann felt a deep sense of spiritual peace after this release. Then she slipped right back into her mother's womb and continued with the regression. She reported:

I'm in my mother's womb again. I lose myself in the feeling of floating. I'm a tiny group of cells, and I'm exploring this huge space in the womb. I'm turning, flipping, and floating freely. I feel free in this endless space. I'm comforted by the feeling of being free to float.

I'm aware of a huge white angel with me in the womb. He's a big white being, and I can see the top of his wings sticking out above his head. I'm being flooded with Divine Light from my angel. I've never felt so much love. My heart is full of spiritual love. My angel is guarding me from my mother's toxicity. I have some wounding from her negative thoughts, but the angel put a shield around me, so they mostly bounce off without much effect. I feel physically protected from the seeds of bitterness she is trying to implant in me. I feel protected from the energy of her hate and grief.

I can see and feel the golden shield the angel has placed all around me. It's like an eggshell of golden fluid energy; but it's

so strong, not fragile like we think of an eggshell. It's so beautiful to see. This liquid sparkly gold field of spiritual energy is
all around me in the womb. I still have it as an adult. When
I close my physical eyes, I can see it with my soul eyes. It has
always been part of me.

At first glance, Luann's experiences in the womb seem exaggerated, unreal and hard to believe. Perhaps you, the reader, are
doubting her experience and wondering if any of this could be true.
As our weekly sessions continued, Luann shared more and more
evidence that her prenatal memories were accurate.

Luann reported this story about Ann, her biological mother.
During her teen years, Ann had a dream to become a nun. That's all
she wanted to do with her life. However, Ann's mother was very controlling and forbid her daughter to follow that path. This controlling
mother then insisted her daughter marry instead. So, under duress,
Ann married Luann's father and immediately became pregnant.

Ann believed the baby in her womb was a boy and was filled
with joy knowing she was going to bring a boy into the world.
Then the unthinkable happened. Ann miscarried at three months
and became consumed with grief. She never healed from this trauma and carried her devastating heartache to her grave. Ann turned
to alcohol to deaden her pain. As the years went by, she became
a flagrant alcoholic. Luann remembers her mother being drunk at
ten o'clock in the morning. This wounded mother turned her grief
into rage and spent the rest of her life spewing anger and hate at
anyone within range, including her husband and their four children born after the miscarriage.

Ann discovered she was pregnant again just a few months after
she miscarried the baby boy she cherished. She was not happy to
be pregnant; but if this was to be, then at least she wanted another
boy. Ann felt betrayed by God when she birthed a baby girl. She
named this baby Luann. Ann never did open her heart to this child

who was not the boy she wanted. One of Luann's earliest memories is her mother attacking her for being alive.

> My mother repeatedly screamed at me, "The good baby died, and I got you. You're bad. He's good. You were so much like a devil you were born with a tail."

> As a child I did not believe my mother. I spent hours looking at the top of my butt in the mirror trying to see if there was a scar from the tail removal. I was never looking for a tail. I was looking for the tail removal scars.

Luann grew up with physical, verbal, and emotional abuse of the worst kind. Her abuse story is one of the worst stories I've heard in my 40 years as a therapist. She shared these memories from her childhood:

> I remember at about age three we were in the grocery store, and I saw the word "Biz" on a box of detergent. I'd seen the ad on television, so I knew how to pronounce the word. I was so proud as I called out the letters, "B - I- Z. That says Biz." My mother immediately pulled me out of the shopping cart and started beating me right there in public.

> My mother used to scream at me for hours. "Ever since I had you, nothing goes right in my life. You ruined my life. Nobody cares about me. They only care about you. You are too smart. You make me look stupid."

> When I was seven, this big tall white angel appeared in my bedroom. Somehow, I knew it was a male angel. He had these huge wings and a yellowish glow about his face. He didn't speak to me; he just stood silently next to my dresser until I

got into bed. Then he would lie on his back right next to me through the night. He was so tall his feet would hang out at the end of my bed. He didn't seem to mind. He was always gone in the morning though I never saw him leave. He came to me every night for a whole year.

My mother could not see my angel. I talked about him all the time. I don't know if she believed me or not. Every night as I went to bed, I would lay on the far side of my mattress, clear against the wall, leaving space for my angel. Upon seeing me do this, my mother would become incensed and drag me by my hair into what I considered the angel's space. This went on every night for a year.

Looking back on this as an adult, I've realized I purposely taunted her by putting myself by the wall. I deliberately let her see what I was doing. It seems I was waving a red flag in front of a bull. Obviously, I was not afraid of the bull. Why didn't I just wait until she left and then make room for the angel? I would not allow myself to be her victim; I did not fear her and provoked her continuously. Every night my sister begged me, "Move over. Move over, she's coming." No matter what she said, I refused to do it. My fighting spirit would not be tamed. I had to constantly fight her to keep whatever power I had in this crazy family.

My angel, who came to me for a whole year, made me feel so special. For the first time in my life, I felt protected from my mother's craziness. Then we moved to a new house, and I never saw him again. He just disappeared. Of course, I was devastated, but I hung onto my memories of his nightly visits.

Now as I'm telling you about my angel at age seven, some-thing just occurred to me. The angel that was present for that whole year is the same angel who appeared when I regressed back into the womb. They look exactly alike, big, white, male, with those angel wings arching above his head. WOW! I just got it. This is my guardian angel! He's the reason I'm a sane, functioning adult. He's been protecting me my whole life. Such a revelation. It's a bit shocking for me to put it all together.

Luann had been seeing me for weekly two-hour sessions for about a year. She was making great progress each week. I spent hours sitting next to Luann on a small couch, sending Divine Light/Love energy into her heart. Sometimes we did the energy work on my healing table. Of course, I was also inviting Spirit to assist with our healing sessions. Often Spirit would appear in some way and create a miracle healing that I could not predict or explain. Luann described one of these miracles in her own words:

Dr. Sher and I were sitting on her little couch. We were both visualizing the sparkling energy of Divine Love filling my heart. The light was pouring in, and I felt myself uplifted into a high-er frequency. Suddenly my mother's spirit spontaneously ap-peared in front of me. We did not call her in; she just appeared. She was luminous and glowing from the inside out. This inner spiritual light also made her skin and hair glow. Even her eyes were sparkling. She was looking at me with this beautiful smile. I'd never seen her look at me like that her whole life here on Earth. My mother spoke these words to me: *I'm sorry for the way I treated you your entire life.* This apology from my mother's spirit changed me at the core of my being.

I felt the energy of forgiveness flow through me without even thinking about it. In an instant, my heart was filled with soul love for my mother. For the first time ever, my heart was filled with compassion for this soul who gave birth to me. I suddenly could see she had a tragic life, and her heart was completely closed to receiving love—from Spirit, from any human beings or herself. I still remember those abusive incidents, but I have only love and compassion in my heart for her.

Remembering any of the abusive things she did or said no longer ignites an emotional charge within me.

I received the gift of forgiveness for my mother from beyond the grave.

This healing from beyond the grave was an incredible miracle and a gift from Spirit that keeps on giving. I am forever changed into a more kind, compassionate, and gentle person. I had spent my whole life provoking people to prove my power and my strength. One of my spiritual therapists always called me "The Bodhisattva Bitch." She saw me as a kindhearted healer who did not take any crap from anybody. She liked this about me. After my mother's apology, I lost my need to be the bitch. I no longer needed to prove my power and strength to other people.

An unexpected miracle was gifted to me by Spirit in another one of my weekly healing sessions with Dr. Sher. She did some energy work that raised my frequency, so I was lifted into the light. I felt myself drift through a doorway into the Spirit World. I knew immediately I was on the other side. I found myself floating in this peaceful loving energy.

Within seconds I felt the presence of a baby. The baby spirit was composed of fluffy cloud-like energy—mostly white with gold sparkles. I could sense the baby's male energy. I felt my heart expanding as I was embraced by this loving male energy. I knew this was the spirit of my brother, the baby my mother miscarried. He sent me this message:

My soul purpose was to bring love to our mother. We had the same mission, and we both failed. We couldn't get through the energy of her negative thoughts. I've tried to contact our other siblings, but they are all completely closed. They don't see me or hear me. It's such a joy you can hear me and see me. It's enough for me to be here with you. I want you to know I've been with you your whole life. I saw everything she did and said to you. I love you. I'm here to help you heal.

Suddenly I knew why I yearned for an older brother my whole life. He was there in spirit, and I unconsciously felt his presence. I thought about having a brother every day. I always thought my whole life would have been different if I had an older brother to smooth the way.

He appeared to me in this session as a little baby. However, I know he's not a little baby. He's a big powerful soul. Our mother inflicted a very deep wound in my heart with her vile messages of loving him and hating me because I wasn't him. He spontaneously came with the gift of healing that deep wound. Now he and I can love each other at the soul level. We can share love even though I'm in the human world, and he's in the Spirit World. Now I have the brother I always wanted. He's in my heart forever.

My angel tells me my soul had a mission before coming to Earth. My soul mission was to bring happiness and joy to my family. I came to teach them love. I wanted to bring happiness to this very sad woman. Sadly, I could not achieve this goal while we were together here on Earth. She was powerful enough to block everything I tried to do. Then much to my amazement, Spirit helped me accomplish my mission when my mother's soul told me she was sorry.

I have discovered I have five generations of prenatal wounding in my family. The wounding comes from the generational pattern of negative emotions and pervasive negative thoughts while the next generation is developing within the womb. I know for sure my grandmother, my mother, myself, my daughter, and my grandson all suffered or are currently suffering from prenatal wounding.

While our daughter was in my womb, my husband's mother died. My husband and I were both filled with grief. Now I know this intense energy of grief permeated my daughter's developing baby cells. She has suffered with deep depression as well as severe anxiety her whole life. Little did I know it started in the womb. Then she married an abusive man who emotionally abused her while my grandson was in the womb. It breaks my heart to know my beloved 11-year-old grandson also has prenatal wounding.

While working with Dr. Sher, my mother and I were the only ones of five generations who have found a way to heal our family pattern of prenatal wounding. You may remember my mother received a healing after she passed to the other side. She is at peace now. My intuition says this family pattern goes back even further than my grandmother. Who knows how many generations back it goes?

I decided I needed help to find a way to do this generational healing so all my ancestors can be at peace like my mother and me. My friend Edna is another victim of prenatal wounding of the severest kind. Her mother was raped, and Edna was the product of that rape. From early childhood, Edna's mother became vicious and hateful to Edna—like a mad dog. Edna was told the rape story over and over again as a child; and her mother continues to harp about her burden of having to give birth to Edna. This unhealed mother is now 83 years old and continues her rant to this day.

Edna is a highly talented Reiki Master. She is a powerful healer and even calls herself 'Spirit Lady.' The two of us and my mentor, Magdalana, have been doing long distance spiritual healing together for many years. Edna and I felt inspired to work energetically to clear our ancestors of their prenatal wounding. We raised our vibration with prayer so we both ascended into the light. Of course, Magdalana's spirit was present and assisting.

From that holy place, we both opened our hearts and opened ourselves to the forgiveness found waiting in our souls. We felt the forgiveness energy instantly flow in both directions— back to our ancestors and forward to our descendants. We both knew it was complete. We didn't have to pray about it or repeat this process. It was done.

Now I can truthfully say to God and the angels, "This pattern of prenatal wounding stops with my grandson!" I intend to make this happen by teaching my grandson and his future wife to surround their unborn baby with Divine Light/Love. Then our future generations will all be radiant babies. This vision of the future makes my heart sing!

SPIRITUAL DISCUSSION

It has been an honor and a joy to do weekly healing sessions with this amazing woman who is so spiritually gifted. Jesus once said, "For where two or three are gathered together in my name, there am I, in the midst of them." Whenever Luann and I gathered together for a healing session, we were assisted by Jesus, Mother Mary, angels, and the spirits of Luann's deceased loved ones. My spirit guides, the angels that work with me, and the spirits of my deceased loved ones were also present. Our combined human energies and the added spiritual energies opened the door for all the miracles to unfold.

Luann originally came to me for help with her brain damage. We used the Divine Light to create the miracle of healing for her brain. My husband is a neuropsychologist, and he could see the improvements in her brain waves over time. Luann raised her vibratory frequency when she healed her own prenatal wounding and filled her heart with forgiveness for her mother. Then she and Spirit created a generational healing for her ancestors and her descendants. This generational healing is the culmination of all our work together. My hope is thousands of families can create this same generational healing. Imagine the big shift on the planet when this happens! The frequency of Planet Earth will be raised, and there will be more spiritual light on Planet Earth.

Chapter Summary

The stories in this chapter beautifully illustrate my strategy for healing prenatal wounding. Essentially, I use the same basic structure for each healing session: open the heart, release the pain, and fill the heart with Divine Light/Love. This creates sacred space for a spontaneous shift in consciousness to occur. Within this structure, each session or on-going healing journey is unique because each client is a unique soul who presents distinct details of the prenatal wounding experience.

I also expect during our session or repeated sessions, each client will experience a spiritual awakening, raise their vibratory frequency, and live at a higher level of consciousness after our work together. **I trust that I can guide each soul who comes to me to transform their life tragedy into a journey of spiritual evolution. This is the key element of Radiant Heart Healing.**

It is a given each client needs to release the devastating pain of feeling unloved and rejected as a baby in the womb. As you've read in these stories, I have three different ways to accomplish this. Sometimes the release is achieved by encouraging the person to cry—not just a little bit, but cry deeply from the core of their being. Another release technique is to have the person give the pain a color and imagine that color flowing out from every cell where the energy of the emotional pain has been stored. The third way is to do toning, which is encouraging the person to make a very loud wailing sound to accomplish the release. All three methods are effective; I intuitively choose the one that is easiest for the client.

After the release it is absolutely essential to fill the client's heart with Divine Light/Love. This is always a key element for Radiant Heart Healing. The Divine Light/Love can flow into the client's heart from my guidance, or it might flow in from an angel or Mother Mary, from the birth mother during a Healing Back in Time, or from a substitute mother during a Healing Back in Time.

I expect all of my clients to achieve a shift in consciousness during our healing sessions. The energy of emotional pain stored in the client's cells seems to be a glue that keeps the old beliefs trapped in the person's consciousness. The release experience dissolves the glue, and then the person is free to make a spontaneous re-decision that is life changing. These stories repeatedly illustrate people shifting from *I am not lovable* to *I am lovable.* Another common shift is *I don't want to be here on Earth* to a joyful announcement *I want to live!*

A shift in consciousness comes easily after processing emotional pain through the heart. It is not a shift that can be reasoned or intellectualized in the mind. You can't think your way out of it. You have to feel your way out of it. During the regression into the womb, the pain of rejection comes bubbling to the surface and is then released. The glue holding the original harmful decision is dissolved, and the shift happens effortlessly. My clients often say, "I think and feel so differently now. I don't even recognize that person I used to be."

After reading these stories you might be wondering if you have prenatal wounding. Sometimes, just recognizing the original trauma brings healing. You might also want to seek out a spiritual healer who is trained in Radiant Heart Healing. See my website (RadiantBabies.com) to find a list of certified practitioners.

CHAPTER THREE

HEALING THE VANISHING TWIN SYNDROME

I am an identical twin, so these vanishing twin stories are very dear to my heart. My twin did not vanish. She was born very much alive. We looked so much alike; my parents could not tell us apart. Only my brother, who was 11 months older, could distinguish who was who. We had an uncle who got so tired of being wrong, he said, "I'm going to call each of you Karon-Sharon." True to his word, he used this name the rest of our lives. Of course, we did the fun thing of switching on our dates. They never figured it out. However, we had a rule: you couldn't go home with your sister's boyfriend. Of course, no kissing either. We had to switch back before the night was over. Our dates probably wondered why these twins had to go to the ladies' room so often.

My twin and I were bonded so tightly, we operated as one person. My mother said we had our own language as toddlers. I don't remember that, but I believe her. We had a psychic connection, so we were always in tune with each other. We each knew what the other one was thinking and feeling. At the time, I didn't think anything about our bond. It was there from the beginning. It's all I ever knew.

We took all the same classes in school, including college. We studied together with the goal of both of us being the best in the class; yet we had no sense of competition with each other. My twin and I discussed everything, and together we came up with a strategy for solving any problem. We even had a double wedding! We never planned that during our childhood; we just happened to fall in love and be ready to marry at the same time.

We were forced to individuate after we married. My twin and her husband moved to California right after the wedding. My husband and I stayed in Indiana. It was one of the worst times of my life. Being without my other half was excruciatingly painful. My heart ached to feel our twinness once again. I actually felt like my twin died, and I wanted to die, too. I felt alone and abandoned. I found myself unconsciously searching for her in a crowd. I discovered I didn't know how to operate in life as a single person. Of course, she had all the same thoughts and feelings. Thankfully, she returned to Indiana after a year.

In our early thirties, my twin was diagnosed with multiple sclerosis. She was living back in Indiana, and we were only 20 miles apart. I began having physical symptoms that didn't make sense. It took me weeks to figure out I was so psychically connected to my twin that I manifested her MS symptoms.

She called one day saying, "I have a new MS symptom."

I answered, "Let me tell you what it is. Your left leg is numb, and it's been numb for two weeks."

She gasped, "How do you know that?"

I explained, "I know because my left leg has been numb for two weeks!"

Strangely, my symptoms would go away once we spoke about it. Her illness was the catalyst for me to create the first holistic medical center in the Midwest in 1984.

We were 62 years old when my twin transitioned to the other side. I had been grieving the loss of my twin throughout her illness, so I didn't have the usual grief trauma most surviving twins experience when their twin dies. Of course, we still had our psychic connection. She was in her daughter's care near Chicago the day she passed. I was doing spiritual healing in California. At 6 a.m., I woke up and felt this urge to call my niece. She answered, "I can't talk. Mom is dying right this minute."

Then I knew why I had the urge to call. Within hours I began receiving messages from my twin's spirit. Often, they were full of humor—that was her personality here on Earth. We still communicate. She's often in my dreams where we continue to operate as one being. After these dreams, I feel our souls still connected in our twinness.

Vanishing Twin Syndrome: A Very Real Phenomenon

More often than we might think, a pregnancy begins with two embryos present, and then one simply vanishes, usually with no physical evidence that the lost twin even existed. This has been documented repeatedly with ultrasounds showing two babies in the womb, then months later showing only one baby remaining. This is called the Vanishing Twin Syndrome.

You might be one of those surviving twins and not know it because the womb memories are stored deep in your unconscious. Some researchers of this syndrome report one in eight single births started with two embryos, and as the pregnancy progressed, one of the embryos simply vanished. That's 12% of single births! I find this to be a remarkable statistic. This percentage will undoubtedly become even higher as medical practitioners become more sophisticated in the use of ultrasounds. Embryos can then be discovered even earlier.

We can explore the Vanishing Twin Syndrome from three different perspectives. First is the physical perspective, which is a purely biological view. This is the domain of medical doctors and scientists. Second, we can view this syndrome from the perspective of the mental and emotional impact on the surviving twin.

This work is usually done by specially trained psychologists, family therapists, or hypnotherapists. As you will see in the following stories, there is a major impact on the mental and emotional aspects of the surviving twin.

Third, we can also view the Vanishing Twin Syndrome from the spiritual perspective. This work is the focus of spiritual healers, energy workers, spiritual mediums, psychics, and some very sensitive surviving twins. Many healers working at the spiritual level can see and communicate with the spirit of the twin that vanished. That spirit twin is alive and well on the other side and usually becomes a spiritual guide for the surviving twin. I, along with other spiritual healers, hold the belief the souls of both twins had a soul agreement to bond in the womb for a short time, and then one would leave and the other would stay. The goal of this agreement is the surviving twin will be highly intuitive and receive guidance from the spirit twin on the other side. The ultimate goal is for both twins (one in body and the other in spirit) to work together so they bring more Divine Light into the planet and raise the vibration of Planet Earth.

I have a doctorate in clinical psychology, so I am trained to work with the mental and emotional aspects of the surviving twins. After completing my doctorate, I evolved into a spiritual healer, so I also have the skills to work with the surviving twin at the spiritual level. As you will see in these stories, I focus on regressing the surviving twins back into the womb so they can feel the love bond first and then re-experience the twin leaving. This leaving produces extreme grief that has to be released. Then I help the surviving twins raise their vibration and connect with the spirit twin who is alive and well on the other side. Feeling the soul love from the spirit twin, both in the womb and then later in the Spirit World, is the key to completely healing the emotional trauma experienced by the surviving twins.

You might be wondering if you had a twin who vanished while you were in the womb. Here's a list of common symptoms for the surviving twins. Take a look and see if you have any of these indicators:

- A lifelong feeling of searching for something that is missing
- Eating disorders: anorexia, bulimia, or overeating
- Unexplainable feelings of loss, grief, and depression
- Extreme sense of loneliness—difficulty being alone
- Having an imaginary playmate who looks identical
- Obsession about twins
- Deep seated anger that doesn't go away with talk therapy
- Difficulty with boundaries—desire to be with their partner all the time
- A deep fear of abandonment

Also, notice your emotional reaction as you read these stories. If you have a deep emotional response to a story, that may be because you have had the same experience.

Sharing the Deep Soul Love of Twins

Pamela came to me searching for a solution to her lifelong major depression. She was 65 years old when she saw me and had been depressed her entire life. I listened to her story for a very long time—like 45 minutes instead of my usual 15-minute intuitive diagnosis. Internally, I was so frustrated I could not find the key for this person. I kept asking Spirit to show me the original cause of Pamela's depression. After 45 minutes, I finally got this inspired thought. *This woman has a vanishing twin that has never been diagnosed.* I was so thrilled I actually shouted out, "You had a vanishing twin in the womb!"

Of course, Pamela looked totally mystified. However, when I explained the vanishing twin theory to her, she got goose bumps everywhere. Then she knew it was true. She sat stunned and silent for some time. Then she said, "I've seen this vanishing twin of mine all through my childhood. She was always there as my playmate, and then she left. I've searched for her forever."

Searching for the Missing

Pamela shared her life-long journey of searching for the missing:

"I can't find it!" It's been a forever thought that haunts my every waking hour. There's not a moment in my sixty-five years without this uncontrollable thought running through my mind. I have this pervasive feeling I'm missing something, and there's such a yearning within me to find "it" even though I haven't a clue what "it" is. I don't know if "it" is a person, a place, or a thing. This yearning has caused my heart to ache with an emptiness that is painful beyond words. It has always been so for me; I was aware of the yearning before going to school. Because of all this, my heart is filled with the deepest grief a human being can experience.

Even as a child, I repeatedly said, "I don't want to be here." I meant, "I don't want to be in this life because it's too hard." As an adult, my mantra became, "I don't want to live in this world." I've had suicidal thoughts my whole life.

As a child I had a friend I called Heidi. I'm not sure exactly when she came into my life or when she drifted away, but I distinctly remember playing with her from the time I was a toddler until I was 11 years old. She was always there—

like before I can even remember. We climbed trees together, played in the hideout in the family tree house, did all kinds of kid things, and talked about everything. As a child I loved the outdoors and especially the stars. Many nights Heidi and I would spread a blanket on the beach near the Golden Gate Bridge and spend hours looking at the night sky and the stars. How I loved the stars! We talked about the beauty of the stars and imagined things about the stars. Together we wondered what was beyond the stars. Heidi was my constant companion, at least whenever I was alone. She was never around when I was at school or playing with other children.

It seemed very strange to me nobody else could see or hear Heidi. I'd be playing in the tree hideout laughing and talking with my friend. My sister would climb up the ladder and ask, "Who are you talking to?" I'd say, "It's Heidi." She'd say, "But there's nobody here." And I'd say, "Yes, she's right there." No matter what I said, my sister could never see or hear my little friend.

My parents became very enraged whenever I talked about Heidi. They said things like:

> "She's not real. She's imaginary.
> If you don't stop this, you'll be taken away to a bad place.
> You're going to hell for this."

I so resented them for saying such things. I could not for the life of me understand why they were so upset. No matter what they said, Heidi stayed with me; however, I quickly learned to stop talking about her.

As an adult looking back on those times, I realize I never saw Heidi in human form. That did not occur to me as a child. She was made of this mystical see-through light, and within this light there was a face that was rather misty and vague. She had long flowing hair like mine and her bangs were cut exactly like mine.

Pamela's Healing

I explained the theory of vanishing twins and how we could heal the pain from that experience. Sitting close to Pamela, I directed her to regress back to being a baby in the womb. She was able to do this quite easily. Then, we went back to that time when the twins were together in the womb. Pamela felt the deep love they shared at that time. She was very emotional while doing this. It was a very sacred moment. She had tears of joy flowing down her face.

I asked her how she felt being with her twin. She answered, "Safe. Loved. Whole. Deep spiritual peace." At that very moment, Pamela was surrounded with a glowing purple energy that filled the whole room. Whenever that purple energy comes, I know my client is in a state of deep spiritual peace. I smiled to myself, knowing Spirit just sent us a beautiful confirmation. Even though Pamela could not see the purple light, she felt the peace energy flow through her whole being.

Then we moved forward to the time Pamela's twin left the womb. Pamela immediately was filled with grief and a deep sense of despair. We used the Radiant Heart Release Visualizations to clear the energy of these deep emotions that were stored in Pamela's body all these years. We also had to release the heartache she carried about the spirit of her twin disappearing sometime in late childhood. This spirit twin was a companion for Pamela even if no one else could see her. Heidi was a playmate who made Pamela laugh and lifted her above the pervasive loneliness that permeated her life. The loss of the spirit twin as a playmate was more traumatic for Pamela because she had a conscious memory of this playmate. She had no conscious memory of the time her twin left the womb.

Next, we filled Pamela with the energy of Divine Light/Love. The whole room filled with sparkling light we both could see. I kept my hand on Pamela's chest, bringing Divine Love directly into her heart. I also gave her these healing messages:

Look at your life with your soul eyes. Your soul chose this path of having a vanishing twin. Your soul made a contract with the soul of your twin before the two of you came to Earth.

You planned to be together for a very short time in the womb, and then she would leave and become a spirit. It's a blessing you had the ability to see her all those years.

She has been guiding your life even when you could no longer see her. The two of you share a deep soul love like only twins have.

Let's send a beam of love from your heart to her heart wherever she is out in the Universe. I see your pink beam of love. It's luminescent—it has a light shining from within.

That beam of love can stretch forever into eternity. It will never break.

Heidi can send Divine Love back to you. Keep your heart open to receive it. You two are connected forever into eternity.

She never really left. You just couldn't sense her presence as you got older. Ask her to come to you in your dreams. Take time to meditate and invite her to appear.

As Pamela opened her heart and received all these messages, she began to feel that deep sense of spiritual peace once again. However, that blissful feeling did not last long. Pamela had a very important message for me. With tears running down her cheeks, Pamela said:

> Finally, I know my depression was all about my vanishing twin. I feel blessed to know and blessed to do this healing work. I've been taking psychiatric drugs for years, and it really didn't help. I've been to so many therapists, I've lost count. They even put me in a mental institution for several years. That didn't help either. I couldn't shake my desire to just take my life and be done with my forever emotional pain. I have this burning question for you. Where were you 60 years ago? I needed you then.

Spiritual Discussion

This powerful plea from Pamela startled me. I was quite taken back. I remember quietly crying as I drove home that night. My heart ached for Pamela's human pain even though I knew her life evolved exactly according to her soul plan so she could learn the spiritual lessons her soul wanted her to learn.

Pamela's plea also showed me the desperate need for bringing this work to the children who have a vanishing twin. Why wait until they are 40, 50, or 60 years old? We could save so many children from a tragic life of emotional suffering if we healed the pain of their Vanishing Twin Syndrome during their childhood years. Then they could learn their soul lessons without years and years of emotional pain.

I imagine a future time when the majority of people understand the Vanishing Twin Syndrome. The parents of the surviving twin will know to believe their child who talks about an imaginary play-mate, honor the spirit of the vanishing twin, and welcome this spirit into the family. The surviving twins will be honored for their spiritual gifts of seeing and hearing their spirit twin. The surviving twins will never be labeled crazy or punished for their gift of spiritual sight. Instead, others will see the surviving twins as special beings who came with a mission to bring more light and love to Planet Earth.

The Missing Piece to the Puzzle of My Life

Melody worked with me once a month for about a year when I was traveling and doing healing sessions in Texas. This is Melody's story in her own words:

> I am the third daughter born into a traditional upper-class Texas family. My family was and is very close, and has always spent a lot of time together. Having graduated college, I became a professional career woman in the business world where I have been highly successful. I consider myself grounded, very spiritual, and quite successful in my career. I have worked hard at personal and spiritual growth. I do yoga and meditate on a regular basis. However, even with all my efforts, I felt I couldn't get to the heart of a deeply rooted pain that was impacting my daily life.

> When I was 38 years old, my 40-year old sister had a reoccurring dream/vision having to do with our mother and blood. She couldn't put it together, but it kept haunting her. Finally, she asked our mother if she ever miscarried a child when we were little. Our mother acknowledged she had miscarried a boy when she was pregnant with me. She never told me because she didn't believe it would have any impact on me.

My mother explained I was a twin. She lost my twin in the second trimester. She didn't know she was carrying twins, and for about a week, she didn't know she was still pregnant.

When I first heard I was a twin, I was shocked, and then I realized I had found a missing piece to the puzzle of my life. I knew it was very important, but I didn't know what to do with this knowledge. It was like a gem I carried around in my heart.

About five years later, I met Dr. Sher. In my first visit, I explained to her I had a deep anger that sometimes controlled me. I would act out in anger and rage, and I felt out of control. I had tantrums that consumed me as a child. As an adult, I would rage at people for the slightest things, such as yelling at a bank teller for a banking error. I would always feel guilty and miserable after one of these episodes. I've spent my whole life trying to keep a lid on a pervasive sense of anger. I didn't know why it was there, and I couldn't control it or clear it from my consciousness.

When I described this anger problem to Dr. Sher, she immediately asked me about my prenatal experience. I told her about my twin, and as soon as I said this, I knew this was the key.

Dr. Sher guided me back into my mother's womb using Radiant Heart Visualizations. Once there, I clearly felt my brother's presence. I experienced the joy and beauty of our connection, and I felt my great loss at his departure. Dr. Sher helped me energetically release the tremendous grief I was carrying, the grief of losing my twin brother and the grief of my parents' abandonment when they didn't know I was still alive.

After the session with Dr. Sher, I felt more complete, calmer and more in touch with who I am. The session helped relieve my anger in the moment, and over time it has dramatically improved.

Another problem I had in my life was a long struggle with bulimia. Eventually I was able to deal with this on a physical level by exerting extreme self-control. I knew how much I was hurting myself, and I finally willed myself to stop throwing up. I hadn't been able to heal the psychological or emotional aspects of my bulimia, even though I had been through counseling with numerous therapists. I had to employ self-control over my bulimia every day, for many years.

Dr. Sher helped me see my death wish was the root cause of my bulimia. Indeed, I could have died from starving myself. It didn't take much for me to see that, given the suffering that goes along with this disease. From the time I can remember, I would wish I would die whenever I was upset. Why did I wish to die? The reasons are complex, and yet simple. My twin was, again, the missing piece. While regressed back in the womb, I discovered I wanted to die when my twin died. I felt so lonely in the womb without him. I felt totally abandoned and wanted to go back to be in the Divine Light and feel the Divine Love. Now I understand, in my mind and heart, I felt abandoned by my twin, as well as abandoned by my parents who had no idea I still existed after the miscarriage.

In the regression, part of me was in the experience feeling the deep grief and heartache about losing my twin. Tears rolled down my face. Another part of me was somehow 'above,' observing my experience in the womb and getting the insights about how my twin's death affected my life.

Bulimia is also about trying to be perfect to be loved. I was overweight as a child. I remember trying to eat as much as my father. Somehow, I thought this would connect us, but instead I just gained weight. Being overweight in my family was not OK. I got the wrong type of attention and my self-esteem diminished. Being bulimic made me lose weight, and true or not, I felt more loved.

The Radiant Heart Healing sessions helped me clear these feelings of despair and wanting to die. I never got to the core issue before the regression back to the womb. Since this healing session my struggles with the emotional aspects of my bulimia are greatly diminished. I rarely even think about it. I feel much more balanced. When I cleared my grief about my twin's death, I also cleared my despair and my death wish. Then my anger lessened greatly, and the emotional aspects of my bulimia have greatly diminished.

> I now understand my bouts of irrational anger,
> feelings of despair, my death wish, and my bulimia
> were all connected to the death of my twin.

Connecting with the energy of my twin was like a homecoming. I felt so much love. It was a most profound experience. Such a gift! I now have consciousness of something that has and continues to influence my life. Now that I have released the pain of my twin's death, I can feel his spiritual presence and also feel his love and guidance in my life.

SPIRITUAL DISCUSSION

It is very common for the surviving twin to have an eating disorder of some kind. It can be anorexia or bulimia, so the person is starving themselves to death. Or it can be the opposite. Some surviving twins hoard food or have a sense of panic at the very idea of restricting food intake. Many surviving twins are very overweight and find it absolutely impossible to lose weight. Either way, viewing an eating disorder from a spiritual perspective is the most effective way to heal this issue.

Melody was managing her bulimia for many years before we did this regression into the womb. As I explained to her, maintaining control is not the same as identifying the root cause of an emotional issue and clearing it. Think about having a garden. You can cut a weed off at ground level, but then it grows back again. A more effective way is to pull the weed and the root completely out of the ground. Then it will never come back again.

During Melody's regression, we identified her death wish as the hidden cause of her anger and her bulimia. We energetically pulled the root of that issue out of the cells of her body and her energy field. Now Melody no longer has to control her urge to die—it's healed; it's gone. It's been replaced by an inner peace and a love connection with her spirit twin. Feeling this love was the key to her healing. **Love is the most powerful healing force on the planet.**

Now My Whole Life Makes Sense

Marianna did a short phone interview with me before coming in for her initial session. She said, "I'm looking for assistance with my life-long depression and a sense of longing and searching for something that's missing." Immediately, I knew we would be dealing with the Vanishing Twin Syndrome. Of course, I assumed Marianna had no clue about this; it's rare for anyone to know about vanishing twins. As we talked, I silently thanked Spirit for connecting the two of us, and I was confident I would be guided to find the key to her healing.

At the time of this initial interview, Marianna was 55 years old and divorced for the second time. She had four grown children ages 20 to 32. Marianna had had years and years of on-going psychotherapy to alleviate depression and heal her sense of longing and searching for something that is missing. Her sessions had been helpful about other issues, but had not alleviated her depression or her need to search for the missing.

Twenty years earlier, Marianna had a near death experience after the birth of her youngest son. She was given a choice to stay or come back, and she came back to be the mother for her children. "I didn't want another woman to raise my kids. I saw the light. I knew then death is not an end—it's a transition into the Light of God." Like most people who have had a near death experience, Marianna is highly sensitive and intuitive.

I guided Marianna to tell me about her birth story. I was not asking about labor and delivery. Rather, I wanted to know about her conception and whether she was a wanted or unwanted baby. She was born right after World War II. Her parents married, her father went to war, and they split up when he came home. Then they came back together and conceived Marianna. She believed she was a wanted and loved baby.

Dr. Sher: Tell me about this sense of searching for something.

Marianna: I've had this sense of longing for something—missing something—all my life. I didn't know what it was. Since age four, I've been constantly searching for this person who I believed would show up and complete my life. I've looked for this person—as a friend, lover, or husband. I can't figure out why I can't find this person I know is supposed to show up. I've been sad, lonely, depressed all my life, but I covered it with a happy face. People would never guess I'm depressed. However, I know it—I feel it inside. I also know my depression is connected to missing this person.

These statements from Marianna made it even more clear to me she was experiencing the Vanishing Twin Syndrome. I carefully explained this concept to her and suggested we ask her body to respond to some statements regarding the Vanishing Twin Syndrome. This technique of asking the body for information is called muscle testing. I instruct the clients to hold out their arm. Then I push on their arm to test their strength. Next, I say to the clients: "I'm going to make a statement. I want you to repeat this statement and I will push down on your arm. If your arm stays strong it is a true statement for you. If your arm loses strength the statement is false for you." Below are the statements we used for muscle testing. Marianna's answer for each statement is in front of the statement.

Muscle Testing Statements

YES: I have a vanishing twin.

YES: My mother's bleeding was losing my twin.

YES: I've been grieving the loss of my twin.

YES: My spirit twin has been acting as a guide for me.

YES: My twin's spirit merges with me at times.

YES: My twin was a female and now is a spirit with no gender.

YES: We are identical twins—one egg that divided into two.

YES: We are two separate souls.

NO: My twin has re-incarnated.

YES: Our soul plan was for one to be in spirit and the other to be on Earth.

YES: My desire to birth twins is due to my unconscious memory of being a twin.

YES: I can heal my depression knowing this.

YES: I can heal my life-long sense of loneliness knowing this.

YES: I've been searching for the soul-to-soul love I knew with my twin.

YES: We had this deep love relationship on the other side.

YES: We have had past lives together.

YES: We have had at least 20 past lives together.

Marianna was absolutely amazed with her experience of muscle testing. She believed the answers her body gave her. At the end of the muscle testing Marianna had no doubts she had a vanishing twin and this loss was the root cause of her loneliness and depression.

Childhood Memories that Surfaced in the Session

Marianna initially said, "I can't remember much about my childhood." As we did the muscle testing, the memory blocks seemed to dissolve, and she recalled many buried feelings, situations, and experiences. She reported:

All my life I have searched for a person to complete me. With each new person I met, I kept asking in my mind, "Are you the one I'm looking for?" I never gave up. To this day at age 55, I'm still looking for this person. I thought it would be a romantic relationship—never found it. I thought it would be a good friend—never happened. I always have this sense of searching for something I cannot find. It is pervasive and fills me with loneliness.

As a preschool child, I believed one of my dolls would come to life and be the person I was looking for. My mother was very worried about me. If I left the house to go out to play, I would tell her to watch the doll because it might start moving or talking. I truly believed this would happen.

I've always had twins on my mind. I wanted to be a twin. If I got a dog, I had to get two dogs. I had to have two of everything. I've been obsessed about twins always.

My good friend was pregnant with twins. I was irrationally angry and jealous. Why couldn't that be me? I prayed for twins with each of my pregnancies. It never happened. I was very demanding with my prayers. I prayed for two every time!

When my daughter-in-law was hugging her son, I said, "Don't you wish he had a twin?" She replied, "No, I never thought of it." I was shocked because I thought everybody wanted two of everything.

I know my twin's name; it's Julianna! I have goose bumps everywhere when I say that. People spontaneously call me Julianna—it has happened my whole life—even in childhood. Another teacher at school just did it last week. Out of the blue, she called me Julianna. As a child I told my mother I hated my name, and I wanted to change it to Julianna. She was very upset with me about this.

I'm feeling this immense joy! What I always wanted really is! I have a twin! The person I was searching for is not here on Earth. She's ethereal—she's a spirit. That's why I couldn't find her.

I worked at the Edgar Cayce Institute in Virginia Beach where I learned this exercise. Each year on your birthday, you meditate at the moment you were born. Every year when I do the exercise this spirit being always comes. I now understand this is my twin. She is so, so… Goddess! Her presence is so vivid. She is just beautiful! She appears as more than light. She has definite form and this beautiful golden blonde hair. Maybe that's why I started dying my hair this golden blonde color. I have definitely tried to look exactly like her.

Knowing about Julianna is extremely significant. Now my whole life is making sense to me. I had an imaginary play-mate, and she looked just like me. I remember playing with her at ages three through six. I would disconnect from her for periods of time. Then we would re-connect. I'm guessing she was always there, but sometimes I didn't notice her.

I've always felt like I should not be close to others. If any-one tried to get close, I would push them away and shut off my heart. I had this thought that would not go away, "This isn't what I'm supposed to be doing." Now that I know about Julianna, this reaction makes sense because nobody could ever feel like my twin.

I have always sabotaged my success. I almost graduated from college, but I quit. I almost do everything. I guess I feel guilty about becoming successful. Maybe I sabotage my success be-cause my twin is not here to share my joy.

More Muscle Testing

YES: My twin sister in spirit is named Julianna.

YES: That is why people keep calling me Julianna.

YES: My grief about Julianna has blocked my creativity.

YES: Julianna guided me to find Dr. Sher so I could learn about my vanishing twin.

YES: Julianna has been guiding this session from the other side

At the end of the session, Marianna announced, "I haven't been this open to my guidance in a long time. Now I know Julianna is real, and I'm filled with such joy. I'm just ecstatic! Now my whole life makes sense."

> "This is the first time in my life I have been able to feel joy!
> In fact, I never even liked the word joy.
> Others talked about joy, but I could never feel it."

SPIRITUAL DISCUSSION

Marianna's story shows the beauty of using muscle testing to discover the truth about a person's life, including the truth about having a vanishing twin. With each statement, the clients can feel their arm become strong or weak. Then there is no doubt about the statement being true or false. The body doesn't lie; so, by using muscle testing, the body can tell us the truth about the vanishing twin syndrome even if the clients have no awareness of this issue.

Notice Marianna received a healing by just understanding the Vanishing Twin Syndrome. We did not do any emotional release work. However, she experienced a big shift from depression to joy just by discovering Julianna. Understanding Julianna is real and acting as her spiritual guide allowed Marianna to rise above her depression and experience joy. This shift in consciousness will also allow Marianna to live at a higher frequency in the future.

We Came to Give You Our Male Energy

I met Kendra when she attended a class I was teaching on Psychic Development in Texas. At the time she was 56 years old. I knew immediately this ordinary looking woman had advanced psychic abilities. I wondered why she was even taking my class when she could have been teaching it. In retrospect, I know this was Spirit's way of connecting the two of us because we had work to do together. We developed an ongoing relationship. It began as healer and client; then our relationship evolved into colleagues trading healing sessions and working together to heal others. After I moved to Sedona, we continued to do deep spiritual healing sessions with each other on the phone.

After the class, Kendra returned for individual monthly healing sessions. She trusted me immediately and began sharing about her life. I was shocked to hear her life story of on-going emotional, physical, and sexual abuse from infancy to the present. Her story includes severe abuse including some of the worst sexual abuse history I've heard in 40 years as a therapist. Frankly, I sat there wondering how she was still sane and able to function. I was awed by her inner strength to overcome all the abuse and keep moving forward.

Kendra was the first-born child of very disturbed parents. Mom was a physically battered wife until she finally escaped with Kendra who was 8 years old. Kendra's raging alcoholic father started sexually abusing her at a very young age. Mom did nothing to stop it. As a child, Kendra's father regularly held a gun to her head and threatened to kill her. He once pulled the trigger, but the gun jammed. Obviously, Spirit wanted Kendra to live out her purpose here on Earth. In our early sessions, Kendra shared all this without a tear. She was absolutely numb—it was her way of coping. I was guided to use Radiant Heart Healing to assist Kendra to release the deep emotional pain she carried. We did these healing sessions once a month for a very long time.

After growing up abused, Kendra chose an abusive husband and stayed with him for 26 years. Once she became conscious she was a battered wife, she stayed to raise her two children knowing all along, she would leave when the children were raised. She escaped the day her youngest left for college. She left with the clothes on her back. She drove thousands of miles to a secret place where she lived in her car for a year, hiding from her husband who might try to kill her for leaving. This was not an exaggerated fear. He often held a loaded gun to her head when she lived with him. He was just like her father.

Kendra shied away from people her whole life; instead, she had relationships with spirit beings. She could see them and communicate with them. Like many others who have suffered abuse, she developed her intuition and psychic abilities to a very high level. Her first memories include seeing Archangel Michael at her side constantly. As a child, he stood by her bed all night, every night. Kendra could see him and talked to him like a best friend. He kept telling her, "You are going to be OK." He has been her protector always. Others could not see or hear him. Archangel Michael is with her to this day—at age 66. Most people think she's lying if she risks talking about her on-going conversations with an Archangel. Mostly, she now only risks talking about Michael to her friends who are spiritually awake.

Since I also see and hear spirit beings, I found Kendra very genuine and totally believable. At one point on our journey together, Kendra told me, "I scare people with my stories of communicating with spirit beings. In the whole world, you are the only person I don't scare. You understand me." Indeed, I understand Kendra and honor her spiritual gifts. She can see Heaven and Earth, holding both visions at the same time. She's an amazing woman who brings more spiritual light to the planet.

Kendra also has a gift for communicating with all animals. She remembers talking to animals as a little child. She asked them questions, and they answered her. She was free to wander in the woods. She remembers having conversations with a deer. Another time a wild hawk came down to say hello and gently ran his talons through her hair. The hawk never hurt her, and she was never afraid. The hawk was her friend.

As an adult, Kendra never lost her ability to communicate with the animals. She can hear them thinking. She works as a dog trainer. Of course, she is the dog whisperer. The dogs tell her what's bothering them at home and what would make their lives better. Kendra then tries to convey this information to the owners. Some are receptive and some not. Of course, she doesn't tell them, "Your dog and I had a conversation."

Healing Kendra's Vanishing Twin Issue

Kendra described her life to me:

My whole adult life I thought something was wrong with me. I had this emptiness inside I couldn't fill. Nothing could complete me no matter how much I searched. It was a pervasive hunger that could never be satisfied. I traveled a lot on my own. As I traveled, I was always searching for that something that would stop the yearning for the missing. When I was pregnant, I desperately wanted twins. Just the idea made me happy. I was devastated when that didn't happen. I never told

Dr. Sher any of this. We were focused on healing other issues in my life.

One day, while talking about her work, Dr. Sher listed all the symptoms common for people who had a vanishing twin in the womb. I had an epiphany! All the pieces of the puzzle fell into place. I suddenly knew I had a vanishing twin! Now my whole life made sense. I was happy knowing Dr. Sher could help me heal all of this.

Dr. Sher mentioned that adults with a vanishing twin history often have an eating disorder. This was a defining moment for me. As a child, I was severely underweight. I look at pictures from that time, and my bones are literally sticking out all over my body. My parents were so controlling that I rebelled any way I could. Not eating was my weapon to show them I could control something in my life. I didn't know it at the time but looking back, I now realize that I was anorexic until I went to college.

Then I swung the opposite way. I didn't have much money for food, so I started eating crackers and peanut butter—it was the mainstay of my diet. I left college 50 pounds overweight. Then I became 100 pounds overweight after my two children were born. Even now it's almost impossible for me to lose weight. I go on a diet and lose some. Then when I get stressed, I start eating compulsively, always going for comfort food, lots of carbs and sugar. Eating has been a problem my whole life. And now I find out this is common for people with a vanishing twin. I find that amazing!

After hearing this from Kendra, I knew we had to do a regression back into the womb. This was the fastest way to heal

Kendra's need to search for the missing. Here's the transcript of that regression:

Dr. Sher: Be the baby in the womb. What is your mother thinking and feeling when she discovers she's pregnant with you?

Kendra: She's crying. She seems very dark. She's so sad because she knows life is going to get rougher for her. She knows my father does not want any children ever. She's afraid to tell him about me. He wants all her attention. He doesn't want to share her attention with children. She's terrified to tell him. She is already getting abused and thinks the abuse will get worse.

Dr. Sher: What is your father thinking and feeling?

Kendra: When I connect with him, I see red everywhere. He's furious Mom is pregnant. Actually, he's enraged. He's beside himself with rage. The red I'm seeing is the energy of his rage.

Dr. Sher: Be the baby in the womb. What are you experiencing?

Kendra was quiet for a time. Then she shared:

I have this floating feeling. I'm floating in this big expansive space. I like the feeling of floating. Then I realize I'm alone in the darkness of my mother's sadness. I feel very scared and alone.

Then I bump into two other beings who are also floating in the same space. I realize there is more than just me in this space. Somehow, I know they are both male, they are my twin brothers. They are like ping pong balls bouncing around. It's a game to them. My worries go away because we are playing as we all three bounce around. We have no worries because we have each other. My fear is gone. We all know how Mom and Dad are feeling about us. We make up games to get through this time.

I notice they start slowing down. They have also stopped growing. I initiate our games, but they don't respond. Then they tell me, "It's time for us to leave. We came to give you our male energy so you could survive the difficult time ahead."

I feel they are gone. I'm filled with this deep, deep sadness. They feel just as bad about leaving me, but they can't stay. I have such a sense of loss. It's a feeling of desolation and despair. Now I have to deal with everything alone.

Then my sadness turns to anger. I'm angry because the boys left. I'm angry I'm left with these two fighting parents. I'm angry I'm all alone. I see I was angry before I was born. I'm an island unto myself because my brothers are gone. I'm totally isolated and alone in the womb. Now, I feel it all over my body. I still carry that sense of isolation. I've had it all my life.

Now there is no love or nurturing energy for me here in the womb. I'm alone, sad, and hurt. It's not exciting to think about being born to these two fighting parents. Mom is just trying to survive. Dad keeps arguing, yelling and screaming. I don't see a good outcome. Yet, I know I have to keep moving forward. My whole life I've felt depressed, filled with darkness, unwanted and alone. Now I see that's how my life started in the womb.

Dr. Sher: Kendra, you are filled with the heavy energy of grief from your time in the womb. Your sadness and anger are pervasive; the cells of your body are filled with a massive amount of dark energy. We can both see it with our soul eyes. I know you are sensitive so you can also feel it. Let's stop and release this dark energy. Give every cell permission to release it. Imagine that dark energy flowing out of your body.

With our soul eyes we both perceived the energy forming into a volcano that literally exploded out the top of Kendra's head. We could both see the black energy spewing everywhere. After the release Kendra felt clear and much lighter. Her aura became much brighter.

Then a miracle occurred spontaneously. I felt and saw the room fill with this high frequency spiritual light. Kendra could see and hear a bevy of angels surrounding us, and she had a glow about her.

Kendra: The angels are giving me a message. *Even in your darkest hours you were loved by the angelic realm. We were always there watching out for you. We are still watching over you.* Now Jesus is appearing out of the light and he has another message. *You were never alone even though you felt alone.* Mother Mary is here with a third message. *We were always there. You were so sad; you couldn't see or feel us.* Archangel Michael is right in front of me with a fourth message. *Your twin spirit brothers have always been with you. You pushed the memory of them back because the loss of them was so painful.*

Before our work together, Kendra did not remember anything about her twin brothers. The memory of them was far back in her unconscious. Once we brought them forward Kendra was flooded with childhood memories of playing with these twin boys no one else could see. She never wanted to play with dolls or girly things. Instead she preferred playing with trucks, tractors and farm equipment she could share with the twins. They played for hours outside in the sand box. Her mother was always amazed Kendra could play for hours by herself. Of course, she could not see Kendra's invisible playmates who were there every day. One memory that surfaced was not a happy one. Kendra tried many times to tell her parents about playing with the twins. Each time, they beat her unmercifully, so she learned to stop talking about her invisible playmates.

Kendra Shared How She Sees the Twins Now in Her Adult Life

My twin brothers appear to me as two little blonde boys. They tell me to call them Kevin and Kyle. They seem to be two or three years old. They look like little cherubs. They've stayed young as opposed to aging with me. They appear as playful little kids who are always kidding around. They don't initiate conversations; I have to ask them questions, and they will answer. They come and go in my awareness. I know I can always call on them and they will come.

People tell me I have a youthful or child-like air about me. In some ways, I haven't grown up. I've stayed young for them. I see life from their perspective. Kevin and Kyle have a sense of wonder about life. Everything is an adventure to them. I have the same sense of adventure and wonder about life. Even though my life has been extremely difficult, I laugh a lot and enjoy life.

People have always told me I have a lot of male energy. I know I do. I refused to wear dresses as a little girl and hated everything girly. I kept my hair cut short like a boy and dressed like a boy. My mother was horrified, but she couldn't change me. Believe me, she tried. As a teenager I didn't have boyfriends or even have friendships with girls. I didn't know how to act like other girls. As I got older, I continued to pursue a very male path. I worked in the fields with my grandfather, went to college to study agriculture, and became a dog trainer. Everyone thought I was gay—even my parents. I never was gay, but people treated me as if I was.

During my teen years I was very suicidal. My life was so miserable I didn't see any reason to go on. I often thought about suicide but never tried it. Every therapist I've ever seen told me most people with my abuse history become addicts, alcoholics, or commit suicide. I had an inner toughness they couldn't comprehend. Now I understand my brothers gave me all their male energy in order for me to survive. My sheer will to live was knowing on an unconscious level my brothers died for me in the womb. I love being conscious of all this.

Now I recognize I've integrated the male energy of my twin brothers who vanished at three months in the womb. That's why I look and seem so male. They knew my life plan included being alone, feeling unloved, and being abused. They came to give me their male energy so I would have the strength and fortitude to keep moving forward in my life. I remember their words in my regression session, "We came to give you our male energy so you could survive the difficult times ahead." This is our soul contract which we agreed on before the three of us came to Earth. It was all meant to be.

I have my spirit twins with me always. My life is now fuller and richer because I know they are here. I no longer search for the missing because I've found it. This is an incredible relief. I feel satisfied instead of restless. I can be content with what I have. I don't need material things to fill up the emptiness. I now have a sense of inner peace I didn't know was possible. People can see the difference and make comments they like the new me who is calmer and more at peace. My son said to me, "The woman you are now is the mom I wanted when I was little."

I've noticed all these body changes. My body is at peace after doing all the release work. I'm able to lose weight when it was impossible in my earlier years. I'm sleeping deeper and longer. My hypervigilance is gone, and all my life-long flight or fight symptoms have simply vanished.

I've had an amazing change in beliefs about myself—what Dr. Sher calls a shift in consciousness. I no longer think any of these statements are true about me. *I'm unlovable. Nobody cares about me. Nobody cares if I live or die. I'm not worthy of love. I'm a disappointment. I'm an island unto myself. I've been all alone since I was born and will be the rest of my life.*

One of my biggest shifts in consciousness is healing my death wish. I spent most of my life wishing I could die and go to the other side. My suicidal thoughts were the darkest during my teenage years. I came very close to taking my life numerous times, but something always held me back—that something was all my spirit beings—my spirit twin brothers as well as my protector, Archangel Michael. After doing my healing work with Dr. Sher and others, I have a passion for life. It's a zest for life I didn't know was possible. I know I can create a beautiful life filled with lots of passion, joy and love. I know I'm here to be a light worker, and this purpose invites me to awaken every morning with joy!

I've been on a healing journey for the past 14 years. That seems like a very long time, but I needed that much time. It's been a journey filled with earth angels as well as spiritual angels. I've received so much love along the way. I've searched for whatever would help me heal. I've done traditional psychotherapy, spiritual psychology, herbal remedies, frequency machines with a holistic medical doctor, reflexology, and Thai Yoga Massage. I didn't just dabble in these methods for a few sessions. I went for weekly sessions for years.

My energy field is transformed so I now live at a very high frequency. I'm happy inside, and I have a joy of life others can easily see. My heart is full of love from spirit beings, human beings and myself. Believe me, I have transformed myself and my life on this journey. It's a journey everyone needs to take!

I'm getting ready to retire as a dog trainer. I have visions of a new life filled with passion for my new work with loving people surrounding me. My vision is to become a spiritual healer and use my gifts to help others move forward on their own path of awakening to Spirit. I won't be working alone. I know all these spirit beings will be assisting me: Kevin and Kyle, Archangel Michael, Jesus, Mother Mary, and my powerful bevy of angels who are always with me.

Spiritual Discussion

Kendra's soul chose an extremely grim life path this lifetime with numerous challenging soul lessons. She came to Earth to learn lessons about survival, being lovable, overcoming abuse, being alone in the world, healing grief, and using her spiritual gifts to become a healer for both human beings and animals. Here are Kendra's own words describing her soul lessons:

One of my important soul lessons is **I'm lovable**. I now know I can connect with people. I used to only be close to spirit beings and animals. Now I can have people friends and share love with human beings.

Another soul lesson is **No More Abuse.** I deserve love, respect and kindness in all my relationships. I've looked back at the person who stayed in those abusive relationships and wondered, "Who was that woman?" I wouldn't stay in abuse for a minute now that I've healed the belief I deserve abuse.

No matter how rough life gets, **I can survive.** I came through the worst experiences in life and still have a good heart. My mother used to say, "You have a heart of gold no matter what." My message to others is:

> "Believe in yourself. We all have a power within that surrounds us during the worst times. In our darkest hours we have the most angels around us."

Assistance from My Mother's Spirit

LoriAnn Manns (psychicLoriAnn.net) is both a professional psychic and a medium. She splits her time equally between Wisconsin and North Carolina. She is one of the naturals, meaning she's had the gift of seeing spirits and receiving messages since she was a small child. LoriAnn knows doing her work as a psychic/medium is fulfilling the soul contract she made before coming to Earth. This is her life purpose and she is filled with such joy knowing she's on her spiritual path.

At age five, LoriAnn knew she was different from the other kids. Her first day in kindergarten, LoriAnn left her desk and whispered a message in her teacher's ear. "That man wants me to tell you he's going to be OK now." Of course, the teacher was mystified and asked, "What man?" LoriAnn answered, "The one standing behind you." The teacher looked but couldn't see anyone standing behind her. LoriAnn went back to her desk.

Minutes later the principal entered the room. After a private conversation with the teacher, she hurriedly left, and the principal continued to run the class for the day. The teacher returned after two weeks and asked LoriAnn, "Can you describe the man that was standing behind me?" LoriAnn gave her a detailed description and the teacher exclaimed, "That's my father. He died at the very moment you gave me that message. How did you know that?"

LoriAnn often got sent to the principal's office for giving teachers and fellow students messages from spirit beings on the other side. She was always in trouble for this. Her mother advised her to stop giving people the messages. LoriAnn responded, "But they keep telling me to go talk to the people. They want me to do it." LoriAnn was 38 years old before she discovered her own mother was a very talented medium who also began seeing spirits as a child.

LoriAnn shared she had a very difficult childhood with a combination of neglect by her alcoholic mother, sexual abuse by her father from ages 5-15, and the complete responsibility for taking care of her four younger siblings. She had years of psychotherapy before coming to see me. She felt healed from all that trauma. I congratulated her for finding a way to heal all of this and move forward to become a highly functioning adult. This woman had not even an ounce of victim consciousness! She not only survived; she found a way to thrive after all those years of abuse.

Regression Back to the Womb

I intuitively knew LoriAnn had prenatal wounding buried beneath the emotional pain from her childhood. It was just a knowing—I had no factual information to suggest this was true, but I trusted my gut feeling. I asked her about her birth story and discovered there was a mystery about her father. LoriAnn does not look like any of her brothers and sisters. She always had a feeling the man she called Dad was not her real father. Her mother refused to answer any questions whenever LoriAnn asked about her dad. She tried off and on over the years. No answers. It was a closed subject.

I explained about babies having consciousness and asked LoriAnn if she would try a regression session so we could see what was going on when she was a baby in the womb. She was excited to experience the regression.

Dr. Sher: What's your mother's first thought when she discovers she's pregnant with you?

LoriAnn: *Oh, Shit.* She's not sure who the father is. She's looking at the calendar to determine the date she got pregnant.

Then a most unusual thing happened. The spirit of LoriAnn's mother appeared from the other side and said:

I was having an affair. My husband was in the Coast Guard and out to sea when I discovered I was pregnant. Checking the calendar, I knew the man you call Dad was not your father. I met with my lover and told him we were going to have a baby. At first, we were both so happy. However, we knew we could not be together and raise this baby. My lover kept telling me, "We have to get rid of it." We saw a doctor to do an abortion, but he told us we were too late. The pregnancy was too far along. That was the end of our relationship. We saw each other a few times while I was pregnant—in a friendship kind of way only. I always thought my husband knew the truth, but we never discussed it.

Dr. Sher: What did you feel just now hearing your biological father called you an it?

LoriAnn: My heart hurts really bad. I've always felt like a burden in this family. I always knew somehow my parents wanted to abort me. I just didn't know the pressure was coming from my mother's lover. My heart hurts when I think about all that.

Dr. Sher: Go to the moment when Mom and her lover are discussing having an abortion. Be aware of your response.

LoriAnn: How dare you even think about abortion. Fuck you guys. I know I'm staying. Don't even mention abortion to me.

Dr. Sher: What happens next?

LoriAnn: My mother makes a big shift. Now she really wants this baby. I get lots of love from her. Her husband is not happy. He never wanted to be a father. The doctors tell Mom she is having a girl, and she gets very excited. She always wanted a girl. Later she finds out she's having twin girls. She's even more excited. Her husband is certainly not happy about having two babies.

The spirit of LoriAnn's mother intervened again with an announcement. *Your twin died when you were four months along in the womb.*

LoriAnn sat in disbelief. Her mother never told her about her twin who died. LoriAnn seemed rather stunned with this announcement from the other side. She was very quiet for a long while, absorbing this news. Then I took time to explain the vanishing twin concept to LoriAnn. She got it immediately. She had a vanishing twin!

Dr. Sher: Let's regress back into the womb to the time before your twin leaves. How do you feel?

LoriAnn: There's so much love between us. I feel this incredible sense of togetherness. We are very close, very protective of each other. I can see her floating in the womb with me. She's only a few inches long. When she dies, I'm filled with panic. I can't bear the heartache.

Tears were flowing down LoriAnn's face. She was quietly sobbing. We did another process of using Radiant Heart Healing visualizations to clear the energy of this deep grief from her heart. She cleared it very quickly. Next, we filled LoriAnn's heart with Divine Light/Love—she could feel it fill her whole chest cavity. She held this huge ball of white light in her chest using both hands over her heart. During this time of bringing in the Divine Light, LoriAnn was very emotional. Tears of joy were flowing down her face the whole time as she experienced this intense spiritual love.

Dr. Sher: The spirit of your twin still exists as energy out in the Universe. I want you to send her a beam of love that goes from your heart to her heart.

LoriAnn was quiet for a moment as she sent the beam of love. Then she said:

> This is very strange. Each time I direct the beam of love to the spirit of my twin, it goes to Aubrey, my granddaughter in North Carolina. Aubrey and I have always had this special bond. At age four, she told me, "Grandma, we don't spend enough time together. We have to be together. We are twins, Grandma. I had to wait to come back to you." She repeatedly announces, "We are twins, Grandma."
>
> Aubrey has done this for years. I never understood her message. Suddenly it's crystal clear. My vanishing twin in the womb reincarnated as Aubrey. We really were twins—she wasn't making that up. When she was born, I was living in Madison, Wisconsin with Aubrey living in North Carolina. From the time she was born, I felt like I couldn't be without her. After she said we have to be together, I listened to my heart and arranged my life, so I spend two weeks a month in Madison and the other two weeks with Aubrey and her mother in North Carolina. Since I work mostly on the phone, I have the freedom to set up my schedule like that. Suddenly, it all makes sense. By the way, the spirit of my mom is still here. She's smiling. She is reassuring me it's all true.

LoriAnn sat in stunned silence absorbing this information about her biological father and her vanishing twin. It was a lot to absorb. Many of her life-long questions were answered by the spirit of her mother. The secrets revealed from the other side shone a bright light on her history. Now her life took on a whole new perspective. She almost whispered, "Wow! So, this is who I really am! Now my whole life makes sense."

Next, I spent some time teaching LoriAnn about the symptoms common to the adult surviving twin. I explained about the inner need to search for something missing, being obsessed about twins, having an imaginary playmate, developing an eating disorder, and having a deep-seated anger that does not go away with talk therapy. Then I asked LoriAnn if she had any of these symptoms.

Without hesitation LoriAnn said:

I've been searching all my life for something to make me whole. At age four, I would lay outside on the picnic table looking at the stars. I knew that whatever was missing was out there somewhere. I just couldn't find it. My parents would have to yell at me to get me to come in the house and go to bed. My whole life I've been searching for something even though I didn't know why or even what I was searching for. I was obsessed with the searching. I just couldn't stop.

I also had an imaginary playmate. She looked just like me; in fact, she comes to me now in spirit, and she still looks just like me. She grew up on the other side as I grew up on this side. Her name is Lisa. She gave me that name when I was eight years old. I always knew she existed, but I didn't know she was my twin.

Dr. Sher: Your soul and the soul of your twin had a soul contract to come in together, connect while in your mother's womb, and then separate. The plan was for her to leave and go to the other side while you stayed here on Earth. She is one of your spirit guides, and that was the original plan. You have a wonderful talent for being a psychic and a spiritual medium. Your twin on the other side is feeding you information just like the two of you planned.

Dr. Sher: Have you had an obsession with twins?

LoriAnn: Oh, my God. Yes. 100%. When I was pregnant the first time, I wanted twins. That's all I could think about. I had what appeared to be a miscarriage, and the doctor wanted to do a D&C. I said no immediately. It was just an intuitive feeling I shouldn't do it. I went back a week later, and my hormone test showed I was still pregnant. That was so weird; I didn't know what to think. Then they did an ultrasound to see what was going on, and sure enough, I still had one baby in my womb. I was thrilled to know I was still pregnant! Then I knew I had been carrying twins, and one vanished in that miscarriage. Thank God I followed my intuition and refused the D&C. I would have unknowingly aborted my son who was still very much alive after his twin left. He's now 36 years old and I love him dearly. So, my son has a vanishing twin, too. Wow! That's a trip!

Dr. Sher: Do you remember any paranormal dream experiences with your spirit twin?

LoriAnn: Yes, indeed. During my childhood we would regularly meet up in my dreams. We used to fly everywhere together in those dreams. I would wake up and remember flying with her. It was so fun—never scary. Also, as a kid I could levitate only because Lisa helped me do it.

Dr. Sher: Did you have an eating disorder at any time in your life?

LoriAnn: Yes, I was bulimic from ages 11 to 15. My father noticed early on that I always stuffed myself at the dinner table. He often asked, "You're so skinny, where do you put all that food?" Of course, I didn't tell him I threw up everything in the toilet after eating. My parents didn't catch on for years. Finally, a doctor in the emergency room called the game. My parents put me in out-patient treatment, and I was able to stop throwing up. That doctor saved my life. I hated him at the time, but now I thank him for saving my life.

Dr. Sher: Did you have a deep-seated anger?

LoriAnn: Yes, I hated everybody: Mom, Dad, all my four siblings. Mom was alcoholic and totally dysfunctional. So, as the oldest kid, I took over and ran the house, which meant I did all the cleaning, cooking, and laundry. I also was the mother to all my siblings. I got them up every morning for school, packed their lunches, made sure they did their homework. I felt like a slave in the family. I couldn't wait to get out of there. I also hated my dad because of the sexual abuse. So, at 18, I ran away with a guy I just met and married him when we got to our destination. I had lots of reasons to be angry, and now I know I was also angry my twin left.

Dr. Sher: Two more symptoms of the surviving twin are emotional sensitivity and strong intuitive abilities. I don't even have to ask you about those. Obviously, you have both. Thank you for coming today. It was such a joy to work with you. Enjoy your relationship with your vanishing twin! And you can believe Lisa reincarnated as your granddaughter. Lisa's soul has two aspects that can exist at the same time. The aspect of her soul called Lisa no longer has a body, yet it still exists in the Spirit World. The aspect of the soul called Aubrey has a body/personality and currently exists in the human world. Fascinating, isn't it? I love being a spiritual detective!

SPIRITUAL DISCUSSION

I did a phone interview with LoriAnn about six months after our session. She described several important shifts as a result of our work together:

> The twin experience with you was absolutely amazing. It was super validating because all my life I've had thoughts and feelings about a twin—but could never figure out where that was coming from. Now I know I'm not crazy. My vanishing twin

is as real as real could be. I've been talking to her more since I discovered who she really is to me.

> I am so much more peaceful since finding out about my vanishing twin. It's a deep inner peace like I've never known.
> I also have more patience and compassion for others.

Knowing I have a vanishing twin has also helped me professionally. After our vanishing twin session, my confidence in my work as a medium grew exponentially. How fantastic is that! Now as I do my readings, I am totally confident my spirit twin is not only with me—she is merged with me. Her presence helps me blend her world and my world here on Earth. This allows the spirit messages to come through with more clarity.

I Can Sense My Twin's Foreverness.

I spent five years traveling and working in London during the 1990's. That's how I met Sheridan. When she walked into my London office, I could feel her high vibration and immediately knew this very special being had an important purpose here on Planet Earth. As she told me her life story, this intuitive knowing was confirmed again and again.

Sheridan, a spiritual healer who was 70 years old, told me she intended to keep doing her healing work until the last days of her life. Furthermore, she predicted she will live to be over 100. Incidentally, I have the same intention. I also expect to live to be 100 and keep doing my healing work. I hardly ever hear anyone express such an unusual intention. I instantly knew we were kindred souls. I loved her spunk and her absolute joy of being a healer. I also knew she was living her life purpose. Only those who have found their spiritual mission want to continue working until their end days. That's because doing your soul work is such a joy, it doesn't feel like work.

Sheridan's first career was a nurse, and then at age 68, after 51 years of nursing, she felt called to take training in spiritual healing. She is now a Reiki Master and has also trained in Transformational Coaching and Energy Medicine. Sheridan declared, "I am happiest when I am in service to others."

As she talked about her life, Sheridan shared some stories about her healing work. She often works with couples who have infertility issues. Many who come to her have been trying to get pregnant for years. Sheridan is somehow able to assist these couples, and after numerous healing sessions, they announce, "We're having a baby."

Sheridan has an intuitive understanding if both the mother and the father raise their vibration, they can connect with a higher dimension and draw down the vibrations necessary to conceive. They also connect with the divine energy which is far more powerful than earthly medicine.

Sheridan said, "I sit with the couple and ask them to connect with a higher vibration—even if they don't understand about anything spiritual. I leave it to their higher selves to do the work. So, I simply guide these couples to connect with their own spiritual power."

Sheridan's whole demeanor changed when she started talking about her personal life. She described a life of isolation and loneliness. She was born to parents who both told her repeatedly, "You ruined my life." Sheridan was the scapegoat of the family. She tried to be a really good girl to avoid the blame and shame from her parents. It didn't work.

As Sheridan grew older, she developed a pattern of people leaving her. She married an American man who came to live with her in England. He broke her heart with his affairs and womanizing ways. Her grief about her marriage was overwhelming. Later in life, her family cut her off completely. Even her best friend got upset about something small near Christmas time and cut her off with no discussion. This friend just ended their relationship of 10 years. Sheridan said with tears in her eyes, "My whole life I've felt isolated and very alone in the world. I've never understood why." My heart hurt for her, but I had no answers.

I asked Sheridan to describe her childhood knowing the root cause of a person's emotional pain is usually buried in their childhood. Then Sheridan shared a secret she had never told a living soul:

> From my earliest memories, I had an invisible playmate who looked just like me. She wasn't invisible to me; I could see her clearly. I called her Rosie. I could never understand why nobody else in the family could see her. She had blonde curly hair, and she always wore a pink dress. She was extremely real to me. If my mother took me on a walk, I had to put Rosie in the pram so she could go with us. My mother was always irritated by this, but I insisted Rosie go with me everywhere.

> Rosie left when I was four years old. I never understood why she left or where she went. I was bereft. It was such a blow. Then I realized I was on my own with my brothers who taunted me endlessly, a father who was always gone, and a mother who didn't love me and didn't want to bother with me.

Dr. Sher: You had a vanishing twin in the womb! How exciting!

I took time to explain the vanishing twin theory to Sheridan. She was also excited to understand about Rosie.

Dr. Sher: Let's do a regression back into the womb and see what we can discover about you and Rosie. Sink into a deep state of relaxation and find yourself as a little tiny baby in the womb. Now, tune in to your mother's thoughts when she first discovers she is pregnant with you.

Sheridan: She is very, very angry. She's disgusted by the whole thing. She has very negative thoughts about me. *YUK! I already have two little ones. That's enough. I'm powerless and trapped. I'm disgusted with myself that I let myself get pregnant. My life as I know it has ended. I wish I could get rid of it.* I can hear her thoughts. She's imagining all kinds of ways to get rid of me. My heart hurts so much tuning in to those thoughts. I always knew she hated me.

Dr. Sher: What is your father thinking and feeling?

Sheridan: *My life is ended. This is not what I wanted. This baby is going to ruin my life. I'm trapped. I have nothing but hatred for this baby.* He is wild with anger. I always knew he hated me. I didn't know it started so early.

Dr. Sher: Be the baby in the womb. Is your twin with you?

Sheridan: No, she's not here.

Dr. Sher: Tell me what you are deciding about yourself.

Sheridan: I feel this absolute terror. I have so much fear it's overwhelming. I don't know how to cope with it. It's beyond my understanding. *I don't want to exist. I should not be here. I've spoiled everything. I hate myself. It must be my fault. I better be quiet so as not to be seen.* My pain is unbelievable. It's a very deep piercing pain. I have a huge sword piercing my heart. It goes to the center of my being and beyond.

Dr. Sher: We need to release all that anxiety and heartache. Ask Spirit to give you a color and begin seeing that color flowing out of all your cells. It flows into a ball in your chest. Good. Now let's ask the angels to help send all your pain out to the Universe. You send it with your mind. I'm using my hand like a magnet to pull it out of your chest, and the angels are also helping with this release. Great. You released it very quickly. Now let's go to the time before your twin left the womb.

Sheridan: She's here with me. We are so entwined. We are holding each other. We have this heart connection. It's so gorgeous being connected to her in this way. I love her presence. I love touching her. I feel deeply loved. She leaves. I accept it is the right thing. I accept the physical loss. I don't want to let go of her spirit. I have a knowing her spirit is going to stay with me.

Dr. Sher: Let's invite Rosie's spirit to come be with us right now.

Sheridan: She's appearing as a pink rose. She is just so beautiful—a beautiful energy. I can breathe her right into my heart. Her very essence is divine. She is giving me a message. *You have never been alone. I've been with you always.* I'm laughing because I just now got it. She comes as a pink rose, and I've always called her Rosie. She's laughing too. She finds this hilarious. Sheridan muses out loud, "Why did it take me so long to recognize you?" She received an important message. *Helping others was always more important to you. You kept your focus on them. It's time you awaken to the truth of who you are.*

Dr. Sher: I want you to send her a beam of love. Send it from your heart chakra to her heart chakra. She has a heart chakra even though she doesn't have a physical body.

Sheridan reported her experience with Rosie in a hushed voice filled with awe:

She just appeared as a very young child with beautiful blonde hair. Now she's sending this beautiful brown earth energy to me. She says she's grounding me energetically. Rosie has a light within. She has this pink luminescent glow emanating from her heart. It's all around her.

I'm sending a pink luminescent beam of love right to Rosie's heart. I can put my hand through it and it doesn't break. Fascinating! Rosie tells me it will stretch into eternity. It will stretch wherever she goes.

I can feel our direct connection. It's just lovely. We are heart to heart right now. It's like she never left. I can sense her for-everness. I feel our soul love once again.

We both were quiet for a very long time, neither one of us wanting to break the sacred silence. This was such a God-moment. Eventually, Sheridan began to talk about what we both witnessed during this visitation of her vanishing twin.

Dr. Sher: Tell me what you are thinking right now.

Sheridan looked pensive for a moment before she said:

The next 30 years of my life are going to be so rich. We cleared something today that is life changing. The depth of my pain was important. This pain was so deep I could never find help for it because it always overwhelmed people. Now it's gone, and I feel free. As I move forward, my spiritual work will be more pure. My heart is filled with happiness knowing I deserve love.

I want to sense Rosie forever. She's telling me to find a brace-let of pure rose quartz. Not any old rose quartz. It has to come from the earth's heart center. This bracelet is to remind me she's always with me, and she's helping with my healing work here on Earth. I feel so blessed to know.

Before this session I was thinking I should stop being a spiritual healer. I believed for a long time my pervasive unhealed pain has been contaminating my healing work. I felt damaged to the core. I believed I had this smudge on my character that prevented me from being a true healer. It was like a block or a shield I could never clear. Before this session, I intended to return home and announce my retirement.

Dr. Sher: Dear me! That's not true at all. It's just the opposite. Your soul chose this path of pain so you could truly honor the deep heartaches of your clients. It's made you more sensitive and compassionate. You know their pain is real because you have lived it yourself.

Your soul chose this path of having a vanishing twin and living through all the harsh treatment from your family. It was all meant to be. All the souls in your family made agreements before coming to Earth, and they all played their roles perfectly for you to learn your soul lessons. You had a plan to come to Earth, go through a life of deep heartache, and then find a way to heal your pain. Your soul knew this journey would prepare you for your life purpose of becoming the Shaman!

Sheridan: It's so lovely to know I've been on the right path all these years. I truly am here to be the Shaman! I've changed my mind. I'm not going to retire.

Spiritual Discussion

I did a phone interview with Sheridan several months after our session. I asked her, "What changes have you noticed since our healing session?"

I am aware Rosie is always with me, and I no longer have a sense of loneliness. This is huge for me because I've had that terrible loneliness my whole life. Also, I feel amazingly grounded. I feel a deep need to spend time alone in silence. It is a precious time, and I feel no urgency to see what unfolds next on my path.

My brother died a few weeks ago, and I was in charge of the funeral. My family members behaved in their usual critical fashion at times, but it all just went over my head. This is a very big change for me! I didn't feel bothered by their criticisms.

I think your work with the surviving twins is life changing. You really have discovered something very important. I wonder what it might be like if a group of us got together to share our experiences. It would be very healing for all of us.

I was thrilled to hear that our session helped Sheridan heal her life-long sense of loneliness. Enjoying time alone in silence is a huge transformation for anyone. There is a vast difference between loneliness and solitude. Loneliness is the result of feeling disconnected from others—both human beings and spirit beings. A person who is disconnected can feel lonely by themselves or even in the middle of a crowd. When Sheridan sits in silence, she is connected both to Spirit, and to Rosie, her vanishing twin. This spiritual connectedness creates a feeling of Divine Love in her heart and eliminates any sense of loneliness.

I intend to follow Sheridan's inspired idea to create a retreat where surviving twins can share with each other. This would be a very powerful healing experience for all the surviving twins. Thank you, Sheridan, for this inspiration!

My Vanishing Twin Brings Purple Energy

Maria came for her first appointment looking very depressed. She walked with her shoulders sagging, eyes looking at the ground, and no bounce in her step. She was only 35 years old, yet, I had the impression she was dragging herself through life. Maria said she was there about her marriage. However, I intuitively knew she came for a much bigger reason. I also knew she wasn't aware of the reason because it was buried in her unconscious. As always, I trusted her visit was guided by Spirit. I felt this little burst of excitement in my heart as I contemplated what Spirit might have in store for the two of us.

I always check the chakras for each client before I begin working. The chakra in the middle of Maria's forehead was wide open; the spiritual energy flowing out of this chakra made my pendulum spin clockwise like a helicopter blade. I was amazed it was so powerful! This showed me Maria is highly intuitive. So, I said, "Do you ever feel or see spirit beings around you?" Maria answered:

Yes, I've seen spirits my whole life. I've felt this male energy around me since I can remember. As a child it scared me so bad. I used to hide in my bed and pull the covers up over my head. One day when I was older, I prayed to God to let me see this male energy. A spirit with masculine energy appeared at the foot of my bed. He was tall, slender, and youthful looking. It scared me so bad, I asked God to take him away. Then I didn't feel or see him for a very long time. Now he comes off and on. I have no idea who he is or why he comes to me.

One day, a few years ago, I saw this woman walking, actually gliding, down the staircase in my house. It was broad daylight. She was full of light, and it shone all around her. I was mesmerized by her. Then she just disappeared. I never knew who she was.

My grandmother came to me right after her funeral. She was smiling and so full of light from the inside. I suddenly felt peaceful about her passing. She didn't give me a message. She was just there radiating this beautiful light.

Dr. Sher: How absolutely amazing! You have a natural talent for connecting with spirits on the other side. This is a gift your soul brought with you when you came to Earth. It's very important for you to honor this gift. I'm getting the message your soul purpose is to become a spiritual medium.

Maria: Really? Are you serious?

Dr. Sher: Yes, I'm serious. That will unfold later in life. Meanwhile, we need to focus on right now. Let's check your other chakras.

Next, I held my pendulum over Maria's root chakra, the chakra at the base of her spine. My pendulum hung there absolutely still. There was no soul energy flowing into Maria's root chakra. This is the chakra that tells me if the person has a death wish or a life wish. Immediately, I knew Maria had a death wish.

Dr. Sher: (gently) Have you been wishing this life would be over and you could just go to the other side?

Maria: (sobbing) Yes, I've never told anyone. It's my secret. I've wanted to cross over as long as I can remember. I even tried to commit suicide at age 10. I tried to hang myself, but it didn't work. My parents never knew.

Dr. Sher: Maria, you have a death wish. We need to find the root cause of this and heal it. Spirit is showing me this image of you as a baby in the womb. That tells me you have prenatal wounding, and your death wish started in the womb. Of course, you don't remember anything from that time. We can do a gentle regression back into the womb. Your spirit was there watching and remembers everything that happened during that time. During the regression, we can ask your spirit to show us what happened. Are you willing to go back and see what happened in the womb? Maria nodded she was willing to do the regression.

Dr. Sher: Be the baby in the womb. What is your mother thinking?

Maria: *I'm pregnant again. We can't afford this baby. I'm really scared about another child. If I have to have this baby, I want a boy.*

Dr. Sher: What's your dad thinking and feeling?

Maria: I can hear him. He's very loud. He's talking about the money. We are moving. They are going in circles. I can't understand the words, but I know they are fighting about me.

Dr. Sher: What are you deciding about yourself?

Maria: (sobbing) I'm a burden. I've always felt like a burden. Now I know why.

After Maria released all her tears about being a burden, she got very quiet and seemed to be having an inner experience. I sat quietly with her, holding sacred space for whatever she was receiving from Spirit. I gently placed my hand on her heart chakra and sent Divine Light/Love to raise her vibration. After a long time, she began sharing her inner experience. Maria shared in a hushed voice:

I'm still in the womb, but I'm also able to observe myself from up above. I'm constantly moving within my mother's belly. My eyes are open and I'm able to see this profound sadness in my eyes.

I'm aware of a purple energy all around me in the womb. It's snuggly and comforting. This purple energy is up against my mother's tummy. It's outside of her, but it's in the womb at the same time. It's not coming from my mom or dad. I feel the presence of a male energy. I can feel his energy touching me in the womb. I feel him. I'm receiving these waves of energy coming into the womb. He has a radiance. I don't know who this is.

Maria was very quiet for a long time. There was a hush in the room—a sacred silence. I was almost afraid to breathe. I didn't want to disturb her tenuous connection with the purple energy.

Dr. Sher: (whispering) Just be with that male energy. Ask Spirit to let you know who this is.

Maria: He's very young. (weeping profoundly) Oh, my God! I'm hearing he's my brother!

Dr. Sher: Yes, Maria. He's your vanishing twin. I got the same message, but I didn't want to say it. I wanted you to discover that for yourself. Now let's go back to the time when he is still with you in the womb. Again, I held sacred space while she connected with her twin. Then she spoke in a whisper:

We are really little. Very, very little. He's against my back. I feel he's pushy. I feel him leaving. (sobbing) Why? Why is he leaving? Why do I have to live? He's saying, "It's going to be OK."

I see myself implanting and burrowing into the softness of my mother's womb. He did not implant. So, he wasn't able to stay. (more sobbing) Now I see him older—he looks like a human being. He appears about 13 to 15 years old. He's outside my mother sending energy to me. He brings the purple energy. I feel this deep, really deep, peace when that energy flows around me. I've felt his male energy my whole life. I just didn't know it was coming from my spirit twin.

Now I see my cousin. She died last year. She's here smiling. She came to me at her funeral. I could see her near the casket. She's with my brother in the light. She's holding a baby wrapped in a yellow blanket. It's a chubby little boy. He looks just like me as a baby. Oh, it's the baby I miscarried! I can't stop crying. These are tears of absolute joy. She wants me to hold my baby. I'm holding him in my heart. I didn't know this was possible. His soul light is amazing! She says, "You take care of my babies there on Earth, and I'll take care of yours here in the light."

Dr. Sher: This is all true, Maria. I've had others report seeing their whole family together in the light. You can trust these visions and these messages. You can trust this male energy is your vanishing twin. The soul of your miscarried baby is with your cousin, and he is surrounded in Divine Light/Love. He is no longer a little baby. He's a big powerful soul.

While Maria was in the womb, I noted her death wish. However, I did not intervene in the moment because I wanted to keep her in the womb to see what else Spirit wanted to show her. Now I said to her, "Let's do a Healing Back in Time and clear your death wish. You can choose a different mother for this. Who would you like to be your mother?

Maria: My grandmother who is on the other side. We always had a strong bond.

Dr. Sher: I'm sending Divine Light/Love into your heart. That light will raise your vibration so you can better receive your grandmother's love. See your grandmother in a rocking chair. She's so joyful because she just discovered she's pregnant with you. She knows how to bring the Divine Light/Love in through the top of her head, fill her heart, and send that light down into her womb. You are the little baby in the womb, and you can feel this love all around you. You feel safe, loved, and cherished. I'll be your grandmother's voice and give you the messages every baby needs to hear:

I'm so happy you chose me as your mother. I love you with all my heart.

I know you are a soul who has chosen to come to Earth.

You are here to learn your soul lessons. I don't know what those are, but I will support you on your soul journey.

Trust everything is unfolding exactly the way your soul planned. You are a powerful soul who has come to Earth with a mission.

Your soul is bringing you the gift of connecting with Spirit. Enjoy that gift. I have that gift myself.

I'm sending the Divine Light/Love into your heart. It is there, shining like a beautiful diamond with many facets.

You are a radiant baby. You are here to shine your light to others. You are here to raise the vibration of the planet. Your light will awaken many.

Dr. Sher: Let's check your root chakra to see if our healing work has made a difference. Sure enough. Look at the pendulum. It's spinning clockwise and it's very big at the base of your spine. Now you have soul energy in your root chakra. That tells me your consciousness has shifted, and you now have a strong life wish. I'm thrilled for you!

Maria announced with great joy:

> I'm so full of light. I like being radiant! I'm thrilled to know my vanishing twin is with me. I have hope for the future. I want to use my soul power to awaken others.

SPIRITUAL DISCUSSION

At the end of this two-hour session Maria left with a strong life wish. She totally cleared her death wish. Achieving this important shift in consciousness was a team effort with me, Maria, and Spirit all working together. Maria had to be willing to follow my lead and regress back into the womb. That takes a lot of trust. She also had to be willing to open her heart, release the pain of her prenatal wounding, and receive the beautiful messages that came directly to her from Spirit. Maria's gift of connecting with the Spirit World was a key factor in her profound healing experience.

Maria was full of light at the end of our session. Notice she had such joy in being radiant. I could see her joy shining in her eyes, her smile and her whole being. Of course, she liked being radiant. I've had many people say, "This feels like I'm high on drugs—but there's no drugs." Being radiant is available to everyone. It's not just babies who can be radiant. Everyone can learn to bring Divine Light/Love into their heart and allow it to shine forth to the world. Everyone can be radiant and full of joy like Maria.

Maria will need to keep visualizing Divine Light/Love flowing into her heart to keep this radiance. I encouraged her to keep visualizing Divine Light/Love flowing into the top of her head and flowing into her heart. Then she will be able to use her radiant light to awaken others on the planet. This is her soul mission.

Sharing a Forever Love

William came to me seeking help for his life-long anxiety. He also suffered from a life-long depression and recurring thoughts of suicide. He was 35 years old, had a successful job as an accountant, a solid marriage, and yet he was filled with anxiety. He couldn't see any big reason for his anxiety, yet he couldn't seem to overcome it. We explored the idea that it had something to do with being the child of divorced parents and being raised by a single mom. That didn't get us anywhere. We'd been working together for several weeks when he came in so excited because his wife was pregnant. They both were very thrilled about this news, knowing now they could create the family they always wanted.

Several weeks passed, and William had a debilitating panic attack. He woke up in the night with heart palpitations, a cold sweat all over his body, racing thoughts, and the worst fear he had ever experienced. Luckily his weekly session with me was the next day.

As I listened to William, I intuitively knew his panic attack had something to do with knowing he and his wife were having a baby. I suggested that to him, and he said, "No, I'm happy the baby is coming. It can't be about that." I learned in my doctoral studies that raising a child can trigger unhealed issues in either parent. Let's say the parent has some unhealed emotional trauma at age four. When the child becomes four years old, the parent will get triggered and not know why. It's all happening on an unconscious level. Knowing this, I suspected William had some unhealed emotional trauma during his time in the womb.

Actually, I suspected William might have a vanishing twin who left early when they were in the womb together. I began to ask him questions about the symptoms common to the surviving twin. My intuition was confirmed when William answered yes to the following questions:

Dr. Sher: Did you have a playmate in childhood that no one else could see?

William: Yes. Nobody has ever asked me that question before. I still remember him clearly. He always seemed like a real person to me. He even looked just like me. He told me to call him Silly because it sounded like Billy. He was kind of silly; he made me laugh. We played together all the time. My mother couldn't see him, but she believed I could. She played along and even let me bring him to the dinner table. He had a special seat, and we gave him a plate and silver ware. She told me it was our secret, and I shouldn't talk about him to Dad or other people outside the family. So, I never did.

Dr. Sher: Have you had an inner urge to search for something to make you whole?

William: Yes, of course, doesn't everybody? That urge started pretty early. I kept waiting for this person to show up who would be the missing part of me. I hoped each new girlfriend would fill that void. Didn't happen. I thought marrying my wife would fill the void. Didn't happen. I'm 35 now, and I still have this inner need to search for the missing part of me.

Dr. Sher: Did you have a lot of anger as a child?

William: Yes. My mom says I was born angry—I even had an angry cry. I cried constantly after birth. I guess I gave her a really hard time. Later on, I had tantrums that seemed to come out of nowhere. It seemed I had no control over this rage that would just come over me. It seemed to slow way down as I got older.

Dr. Sher: Were you ever diagnosed with an eating disorder?

William: Yes, as a matter of fact I was. In high school I was severely depressed and lost a lot of weight. I got so skinny my clothes were just falling off me. I passed out at school one day and was taken to the hospital emergency room. The ER doctor told me and my mom I was literally starving myself to death. My mom understood this was serious when he used the word anorexic. After a year of outpatient treatment, I changed my relationship with food, and I'm OK now.

William's answers to these four questions gave me enough information to confirm my suspicion. William definitely had a vanishing twin in the womb! I was absolutely sure given his answers. So, I explained the whole theory of the Vanishing Twin Syndrome to him. He looked rather stunned, but thank goodness he believed me. Next, I explained the regression method to him, and he trusted me enough to experience it.

Regression into the Womb

I guided William into a very relaxed state so he could ease into the regression. My heart felt uplifted, and I just knew he would find a healing in the regression process.

Dr. Sher: Be the baby in the womb. Just feel and sense. Tell me what's happening to you.

William: I'm in the womb. I can feel my mother has so much fear. I'm filled with fear because she has so much fear. There's no safe place for me to go. The fear is everywhere.

Dr. Sher: Is your twin with you now?

William: No, I'm alone in the fear.

Dr. Sher: Go to that time when your twin is still with you in the womb.

William: (long silence) There, I found him. I have my twin with me. We just bumped into each other. He's really close. His face is by my face. I can see him clearly. (crying gently) I feel safe with him here. I have no fear now. I feel the love we share. I've never felt so loved as right now. He says, "It's a soul to soul love." I see this light around both of us. It's a very bright light.

Dr. Sher: You shared that soul love long before the two of you planned to come in together as twins in your mother's womb.

William: He just told me we have a forever love. Amazing. I love this feeling. I've never felt this before.

Dr. Sher: Go to that moment your twin leaves. How do you feel?

William: (sobbing) I feel desperate. I don't want to move forward without him. I call out to him, "Take me with you. I can't stay here without you. Come back for me." He can't come back. I just want to die. That's all I can think about. I just want to die. I'm stuck here. I don't know how to leave and be with him.

Dr. Sher: How long did he stay with you in the womb?

William: He tells me he left at the end of the second month.

Dr. Sher: Now move forward in time. You are still in the womb. Your twin is gone. What are you experiencing?

William: I'm filled with fear. That love feeling is gone. I have to do this on my own. I feel very alone. I'm not supported. I'm immobilized with fear. I don't know which way to go.

I directed William to imagine the fear energy leaving the cells of his body. He was very skilled at visualizing, so we accomplished this in about 15 minutes. Next, we did a Healing Back in Time. William was a devout Catholic, so he chose Mother Mary to be his mother for this healing. Next, I guided him through a scene where he was the baby in the womb of the Blessed Mother.

Dr. Sher: See Mother Mary rocking in a rocking chair. She has just discovered she is pregnant with you. She is thrilled to be chosen to bring you into the world. Feel yourself there in her womb. You can feel her motherly love and hear her talking to you. I will be her voice and give you the messages every baby needs to hear:

I'm so glad you chose me as your mother. I love you with my whole heart and soul. I'm here to support you on your earthly journey.

You have come with a soul purpose. I don't know what that is, but I will help you discover your purpose.

I don't know if you will be male or female, but I will love you either way.

Your twin brother will be with you for a while. You two have a deep soul love. He will leave, but know this is the plan. He will stay connected in Spirit.

Know you are loved by God and the angels. It is Divine Love so you don't have to earn it. You are loved because you exist. You deserve love. You are worthy of love. You are lovable.

Dr. Sher: William, tell me what you are experiencing with Mother Mary.

William: I feel safe. I believe her words. The words flow right into my heart. I see a very bright light. It's so huge! It's all around me in Mother Mary's womb. It's the same light I saw when Silly was in the womb with me. (crying quietly) The light and the love are beyond this world. It's coming directly from Heaven. Somehow, I just know this. I want to keep this feeling forever.

Dr. Sher: You can. I'll teach you how. You did a wonderful job of being the baby. Now it's time to come back to the present. Be your grown-up self again. Know you will remember everything that happened during your regression.

Next William and I had a long discussion about the information that surfaced during his regression. I explained he formed a death wish in the womb when Silly left. This death wish was the root cause of his depression, becoming anorexic, and his suicidal thoughts that sometimes surfaced though he never attempted suicide.

Dr. Sher: We healed your death wish when the Divine Light/Love came into the womb and you felt the wonderful feeling of the light in your heart. In that moment your heart was healed at the soul level.

I can teach you to use Radiant Heart Healing visualizations to continue bringing that light and that love into your heart every day from this day forward. You can feel spiritual love instead of anxiety and depression. Then you will be a radiant being filled with light and love.

I want you to bring your wife here to my office so I can teach both of you about the soul plan. The soul of your baby came to teach you and bring your birth trauma to consciousness. Eons ago, your three souls made an agreement before any of you came to Earth. The agreement was you would have a vanishing twin in the womb and experience all the emotional trauma that comes with that soul choice. You and your wife agreed before coming you would find each other, fall in love, marry, and bring the soul of this baby into her womb. The presence of this baby triggered your prenatal anxiety so you would be motivated to find a way to heal it. It is all unfolding according to the grand plan written by your souls.

There's one more part of the grand plan. The soul of your baby planned to come at a time when I am teaching the Radiant Baby Process to young parents. This soul came to you knowing you and your wife would follow the plan and learn to send Divine Light/ Love into the womb.

> The grand plan is unfolding exactly as the
> three of you designed it!
> The soul of your baby volunteered to be a radiant baby.
> Only Spirit could orchestrate such a sacred meeting.

Spiritual Discussion

I always feel so blessed when I see a client's soul plan unfolding right in front of me. I also feel blessed to be included in this soul plan. It was not an accident William was in treatment with me before he and his wife conceived their first baby. It was a soul agreement made among our souls before any of us came to Earth. The Universe brought us together without any of us consciously knowing about this grand plan. Amazingly, we all ended up in the right place at the right time for this beautiful healing to unfold. It was all meant to be!

Chapter Summary

The souls of the vanishing twins and the souls of their surviving twins are a unique group of souls. For each pair, the circumstance of their birth or death was never an accident—it was all part of a grand plan. The surviving twins have suffered greatly because at the human level they did not know their soul chose this unique route for beginning life here on Earth.

Spiritual awakening of the surviving twin is the goal of each vanishing twin soul plan. More Divine Light/Love flows into Planet Earth as each surviving twin awakens and evolves to higher levels of consciousness. Collectively the twins all have the same spiritual purpose. These high spiritual beings have come to Earth to raise the vibratory frequency of the planet. This has always been part of the grand spiritual plan.

In the case of the Vanishing Twin Syndrome, the deepest healing takes place when the surviving twin makes a soul to soul connection with the spirit twin who is alive and well on the other side. During the session I always guide each client to regress back to the womb to the time before her twin left. My client can then experience the twin connection and the soul love that bonded them in a feeling of oneness. Then, as I hold sacred space, the miracle of healing flows instantly into the client's heart, eliminating all human pain. This soul love from the spirit of the twin is a very powerful healing force. It is such a high frequency—such a flow of Divine Light/Love—that it brings a depth to the healing that cannot be attained if we stay focused on the human level of being.

At the end of a vanishing twin session, I have the surviving twin send a beam of love to the spirit of the vanishing twin. Then I ask the client, "What does your beam look like?" The answer might be, "It's rose-colored energy." Then I ask, "Does the rose-colored energy have a light within? Does it look luminescent?" The answer is always yes. That tells me the client is sending Divine Light/Love or soul love—not just the energy of human love.

Soul love is the force that connects human beings on this side of the veil with spirit beings on the other side of the veil. This soul love is a powerful force that reaches across time and space to reconnect the hearts of the spirit twin and the surviving twin. Accessing the spirit twin's soul love is the key to healing the deep pain of each surviving twin.

There are millions of people like Pamela, Melody, Marianna, Kendra, Sheridan, LoriAnn, Maria, and William walking on the planet searching for a solution to their emotional pain that started when their twin left the womb. These millions are calling to me to finish this book and get my message of the vanishing twins out to the world. My soul hears their call. The little whispering voice of my soul is a force that fans the flames of my passion for this work.

CHAPTER FOUR

HEALING SOUL LOSS AFTER ADOPTION

I have no personal experience with adoption. I was not placed for adoption nor have I adopted a child. So, my knowledge about the deep emotional pain involved with adoption comes from working with clients for the past 40 years. They have taught me by opening their hearts and sharing their emotional pain from the deepest part of themselves.

As soon as I hear, "I was adopted," I expect to find prenatal wounding with the client sitting in front of me. The emotional wound might be hidden in the unconscious, but it's there. It's a given that at some point during the pregnancy the mother made a decision, or was forced to decide, to place her baby with another family or with an adoption agency. So, the baby feels the lack of mother-baby bonding from the beginning or feels the mother-baby bond break when the mother makes that decision later in the pregnancy. This loss creates, what I call, a deep soul wound for both the baby and the mother, and sometimes the father also. All the painful emotions generated by adoption motivate both the baby and the birth parents to find a way to heal their soul wound.

I've worked mostly with adults who were placed for adoption at birth and then had to deal with their profound sense of grief, heartache, rejection, unworthiness, not belonging, guilt for being born, feeling less than, and forming a death wish because their emotional pain is so profound. Most seem to believe there is no way to heal this profound pain. They come for counseling expecting only to learn techniques to manage their pain. They sometimes think reuniting with their birth parents is the key to healing their pain. However, the reunion is not always a positive experience. If the birth parents reject the child a second time, it is absolutely devastating.

Some children who are placed for adoption have a great deal of pain about the separation and a deep yearning to be reunited with either one or both biological parents. Others do not seem to acknowledge having any feelings of loss, curiosity about their early beginnings, or yearning to connect with their biological parents. Feelings about being placed for adoption often change over time. Some children seem to have no pain in their early years, and then the pain comes to their awareness later in life.

Each child placed for adoption is affected on some level; however, the emotional issues are very individual and the degree to which it affects the person's life is also very individual. I believe this is so because each person came to Earth to learn unique lessons within the soul plan. When you look at life with your soul eyes, there is nothing wrong or bad in any adoption scenario. Remember, all adoption issues are a blessing for spiritual growth, and they need to be healed with love.

The soul plan holds the premise: *My soul chose this birth scenario so I could learn my soul lessons and achieve great soul growth. My soul wants me to heal my suffering, give up my victim consciousness, and feel empowered to create a life filled with peace, love, and joy.* My clients usually feel empowered when they embrace the idea their very own soul created the soul plan they are now living. In addition to teaching about the soul plan, I also use regression therapy, Healing Back in Time, and healing with the energy of Divine Light/Love. The stories in this chapter illustrate the effectiveness of using these gentle yet powerful spiritual methods for healing the pain of adoption.

I See the Light

Andrew called for an appointment at my holistic clinic in Northwest Indiana. He came seeking help for his life-long depression. He was 45 years old and a very successful professor at a local university with a lovely wife and four children. It sounds like he should have been happy, but he shared with me he had been very depressed his whole life. He covered this well, so his friends and family had no clue he spent time wishing his life was over. He just wanted to be done with the depression and lack of love that had plagued him since he could remember. I explained he had a death wish, and he agreed, although he had never used that term about himself.

Before coming to me, Andrew did some traditional psychotherapy, but had never done anything spiritual, taken any spiritual classes, or read any books about spirituality or healing. As you will see, he did an amazing session given he was so uninformed about spiritual healing. Somehow, he trusted my guidance, and we found the key to his lifelong depression.

Early in the session Andrew mentioned he was adopted—and never met his birth parents. He was raised by very loving adopted parents who provided a beautiful childhood for him and his adopted sister. Logically, he felt he "should be a happy guy" given his childhood was so idyllic. Of course, he had no clue being placed for adoption usually creates a deep prenatal wound that invites the baby to decide: *I am not lovable* and *I just want to die.* As I explained this to Andrew, he nodded and said, "I've known my whole life my heart was closed. I feel unlovable no matter who says, 'I love you.' It just doesn't go in."

I explained how the baby in the womb has consciousness and knows at the soul level everything mom and dad are thinking and feeling. All these thoughts and emotions have an energy that gets stuck in the cells of the little baby body being formed in the womb. Based on this energy, the baby makes decisions. These decisions become beliefs held in the unconscious and become the driving force for the person's life. Andrew was a perfect example of this. His unconscious beliefs, *I'm not lovable* and *I just want to die*, were driving his depression and unhappiness. He couldn't fix any of this because he did not even know he held these beliefs—let alone, how to heal them. Consequently, he was stuck.

I explained to Andrew I could guide him back into the womb with a very gentle relaxation process. There he could experience the original thoughts and feelings of the baby being placed for adoption. He quickly agreed to experience it. So, I gently regressed him back into the womb. He began to get images of scenes while he was in his mother's womb and he received an awareness about his mother's thoughts and feelings. He reported these to me while staying in a regressed state.

Here's Andrew's experience during the regression:

> I'm in my mother's tummy and I know she's very stressed. I can hear lots of yelling and fighting around us. Lots of people are upset with her because she told them I'm here. They are fighting about me. I can hear her thoughts and feelings. I know she loves me. She's scared about all the fighting, but she still loves me. This is amazing. (sobbing) I never knew she loved me.

At that moment, Andrew was overcome with the feeling of love from his mother. Tears flowed down his face as he took in her motherly love. For the first time in his life, he felt the energy of her mother love in his heart. He wept from the joy and wonder of deep love between himself as the baby in the womb and this very young mother who was enduring all the fighting. While weeping, he unconsciously held both hands over his heart. That original experience of mother love was hidden in his unconscious mind. He could not remember it or feel the effects of it until he experienced it again in this regression. Experiencing this scene created a transformational moment of receiving her love.

Dr. Sher: What happens next?

Andrew thoughtfully replied:

My mother leaves to get away from all the fighting. She doesn't know where to go to find a safe place. I hear her thoughts. *Where can I go and keep us safe? We have to stick together. This is my baby and we have this connection.* It gives me hope that she thinks, "We have this connection." I know everything will be OK if we stay bonded together. Then, I feel all this movement and a different noise. It's a very loud noise. She tells me we are on a train to her grandmother's house. I'm happy because she says we. I want to stay with her even though she's scared. She's all I know. I can see her blonde hair and a green coat as she sleeps on the train. Somehow, I'm above my mother looking down at her. Her thoughts are quiet as she sleeps. I like the quiet.

A woman with a very soft voice meets us when the train stops. My mother calls her Grandma. My mother is happy to see her. She feels safe here. Nobody is yelling. I like my mother's happy feelings. It feels good all around me. Grandma keeps talking and talking and talking. She keeps talking for days. Now I don't like this woman. Her talking is distracting my mother from connecting with me. My mother is pulling farther and farther away from me. I feel our connection break! (sobbing) She flipped a switch. She turned off her love for me. I'm all alone in her tummy.

In the moment, Andrew was flooded with fear, hurt, and despair about the loss of his love connection with his mother. The pain of her rejection flowed through every cell of his body. Tears flowed so hard he could not continue talking. It was so real to him—like it was happening in the present moment.

We stopped the regression and used Radiant Heart Healing visualizations to release the energy of all these powerful emotions. I was thrilled because I knew this release would allow for the healing of his lifelong depression. By pushing down these emotions, he kept the energy of his emotional pain trapped within him. I knew we were releasing the energy of his original trauma in the womb. This pain was the underlying cause of his depression and his death wish. At some point, he finished the release and came to a sense of peace. He was shocked when this happened. I wasn't. I always tell my clients: "Underneath the pain is a place of deep spiritual peace." He experienced that peace without knowing I was expecting this to happen.

Andrew was in a place of peace, but I knew we had to continue. I explained to Andrew we had to do a Healing Back in Time—creating an experience of Divine Light/Love for that abandoned baby. I knew it wasn't enough to just clear the pain of feeling unloved. We had to create an experience of love so he could feel his little baby heart filled with the energy of Divine Light/Love. He could also remember the feeling into the future. He needed to experience the energy of mother love, not just talk about it.

Again, Andrew followed my guidance. He chose his adopted mother to be his mother for this healing. We visualized a scenario in which he was born to this loving mother who opened her heart to him. I set the scene for Andrew's Healing Back in Time.

Dr. Sher: Your adopted mother is connecting with the Divine Light/Love energy. She's bringing it through her crown, filling her whole chest with the light, and then sending this Divine Light/Love into her womb. You are this little baby in her womb surrounded in the light. I will be the voice of your loving mother and give you the messages every baby needs to hear:

I love you with all my heart. I'm so happy you're here.
Your soul chose your birth parents so they could deliver you
   to me.

I feel so blessed your soul chose me to be your new mother.
Our family prayed for a baby and you are the answer to our
   prayers.

I'm going to love you and support you on your Earthly soul
   journey.
I look forward to teaching you all about love.

During this Healing Back in Time, Andrew soaked up the love from his adopted mother. He cried gently through the whole experience. This time it was tears of joy because he could feel he was cherished and loved beyond anything he ever could have imagined.

Andrew: Oh, my God! I see the light! I see it for real! It's the brightest light I've ever seen. I can feel my mother's love. My heart is full to bursting!

My own heart filled with absolute joy and wonder at this sacred moment for Andrew. I knew his experience of seeing the light was a miracle moment for him. We sat together in absolute stillness. I needed to keep my joy to myself so I could hold sacred space for this courageous man. I could tell he was reviewing his experience in his mind. We held this sacred space for at least 15 minutes, neither of us wanting to break the God-moment we had created. Finally, Andrew broke the silence.

Andrew: (whispering) I never would have believed this except it is my own experience. I saw and felt it all. I felt my birth mother disconnect, and I felt my new mother open her heart and fill me with the light. I have no doubt it's all true. It really happened that way.

Now I understand my whole life!

SPIRITUAL DISCUSSION

That evening, I had a quiet moment to reflect about Andrew's healing. I felt this intense gratitude that Spirit guided this session, so together, we could assist Andrew on his healing journey. I know I never do this work alone. It's always a team effort with me, the client, and Spirit. Andrew was amazing. He did all this healing work with no previous spiritual training or knowledge. He had such a desire to heal he trusted me and flowed easily with the process. I know this healing session was a moment of spiritual transformation—a defining moment that will change him forever.

One of the most important moments in this session was when Andrew felt his mother's love during the regression. He spontaneously said, "I know she loves me. This is amazing. I never knew she loved me." This shift in consciousness healed Andrew's heartache of feeling unloved. My telling him his mother loved him would not have carried the same healing power—he had to feel it himself. Almost every client placed for adoption has the belief, "My mother/father didn't love me." Sometimes that's true. However, many times the parents really did have a great love for their baby. Out of this love, they placed the baby with another family so their child could have a better life. These parents then have their own deep soul wound—often a forever grief they take to the grave.

It's important to know Andrew's soul chose this path of adoption for his birth. Before coming to Earth, Andrew created this soul plan involving his birth mother, his birth father, his grandmother, and his adopted parents. Of course, all the souls involved in this situation agreed to be part of this spiritual plan. All soul plans have the ultimate goal of each individual drawing closer to Divine Light/Love and closer to the Creator.

Andrew exclaimed, "I see the light." In that moment he had a spiritual awakening, and he did come closer to the Creator. It is part of the soul plan that each person in the adoption experience endure deep heartaches. The person learns his soul lessons when he heals these heartaches. Then the soul plan is complete.

A Sacred Redefining of My Birth

Debbie is a nurse and a spiritual healer with many years of experience working with clients. She is certified as a Reiki Master and a Healing Touch Practitioner. This delightful woman is a very evolved soul who has the ability to see and communicate with spirits. Mother Mary and the angels regularly appear to her during her healing sessions. Obviously, she has learned to pierce the veil between the two worlds. We did this session on her 50th birthday. I've always thought that was orchestrated by Spirit. Here is her story in her own words:

> I was adopted at the moment of my birth. Within twelve hours, the pediatrician my birth parents had chosen, picked me up from the hospital in Denver, Colorado and took me to Greeley where I would live.

> Years later, I would touch back into the moment I was born during a guided visualization experience. This was years before seeing Dr. Sher. I remembered the anguish and despair of those first days, never again hearing my mother's voice or feeling her heartbeat—each moment waiting and expecting to be in that familiar space. As time passed, the rawness of that separation faded into a constant, deep longing for that gentle mother place.

I felt as though I was trespassing in my new parents' home, an unwanted visitor who was bothersome. Somehow there was always a feeling of separation, a need to behave correctly and excel in everything I did so I would be safe.

During a Radiant Heart Healing workshop, Dr. Sher began describing the death wish and explained one cause for that would be separation of mother and child within the first year of life. I suddenly realized every adopted baby has exactly that experience.

A few months later, I went to Dr. Sher for a personal session. I knew I needed to shift the energy of the unwanted child death wish. I scheduled my session on my 50th birthday. It was my birthday gift to myself.

The session began with visualizations for grounding and opening my heart. Then Dr. Sher said she felt the presence of a very, very bright light in front of us, and she was getting intuitive thoughts about Mother Mary assisting with the session. I looked on my mind screen—there Mother Mary was, standing a few feet in front of me, looking at me with such great love.

Then Dr. Sher took me into the womb and asked me to go back to when I was very small—when my mother first discovered she was pregnant with me. My mother's first response was joy, wonder, and great love for me. I could feel it in my heart. Then reality set in. She was coming from a very needy place by the time she told my teenage father, "I'm pregnant." His face went white, he pulled his energy in, and he put up a wall between himself and my mother. His parents' reaction was to scorn my mother and separate their son from us entirely. My mother's parents coldly gave her only one option: To be banished, to give the child up for adoption, and when she had rid herself of this shame, then to go on with her life as if I had never existed. It was a brutal decree.

As the baby in the womb, I was aware of all this. I wanted to leave, to go back to Spirit. I could hear my mother's words and the words said to her. I could feel the energy of my mother's emotions flowing into my little baby body. The emotions around her were so strong, and they were being used as weapons of pain, to manipulate her to give me up. The love bond with my father was totally severed. She was alone and filled with fear and grief. I sensed how powerless she felt, how hurt. I felt her pain and confusion. I felt grief, and guilt that I was there—my presence hurt my mother. I felt I had no right to be here.

I already knew my birth mother died several years previous to this session. Suddenly the spirit of my birth mother appeared from nowhere. We didn't call her; she just came in. She sent me an important message. *I am so sorry for hurting you. I didn't know I was doing that.* I felt the energy of forgiveness flowing between our souls. It came without me even thinking about it.

Then I said to my mother's spirit, "You were not wrong in the eyes of Spirit. You were not wrong in the eyes of God. You were not wrong in the eyes of Mary. You were a perfect expression of love. Your joining with that boy you loved, my father, was a perfect expression of love. My creation was a perfect expression of love."

As I said those words to my mother, I saw the truth. I knew I was created from a joining of their love, and my mother's first thought of me was love. And all else in that moment faded away. In spirit, I went to her, held her, joined hearts with her. We shared this blissful soul to soul love for a very long time. Dr. Sher sat so quietly I didn't even know she was there.

> This was a major milestone on my healing journey—
> a sacred re-defining of my birth.

Then Dr. Sher said, "I'm thrilled you are feeling all this love. We still need to release your grief and the feeling of having no right to be here." She asked me to give all the pain and guilt a color. I felt grey. She directed me to release the grief from that baby I had been in the womb. I felt myself holding that baby in my hands, and as the grey drained from my infant self, tears flowed down my cheeks, and I felt/saw that grey flowing out her feet and into my heart center.

As we started to release the ball of pain and guilt at my heart center, Dr. Sher said, "Mother Mary is helping you." I responded, "No, she's not just helping me. The image I'm getting is that she came to me, put her arms around me, and she's holding me." As I said that, I felt Mother Mary pulling the grief and pain out of my heart. Within minutes it was gone. Dr. Sher said, "Mother Mary told me she's always been with you." I said, "That's the mother love I always felt was there somewhere close; but it did not come from the mother who adopted me."

As I left my session, and moved through the next days, I could feel that incompleteness, that deep anguish I had always felt, that deep longing for my birth mother, was gone. My love connection with my birth mother is a sacred part of me now. In that moment of spirit merging, we both were healed.

The healing energy from my profound session is still moving through me. It's healing so many wounds I couldn't seem to heal before. It seems to be happening outside of my awareness. Now I know it's OK for me to be here, to have my own home, to be wherever I am. I know I will no longer step aside and apologize for being in another's space, or feel I am an unwanted intruder. I will no longer give up my boundaries to whoever is near me, but rather stand strong in my center, peacefully. It is truly perfect for me to check into my needs, wants, and desires and to state them clearly.

This healing session had a surprising effect on my work. I see and feel stronger Divine Love moving through my hands as I touch my clients and empowering my words as I speak. I feel myself truly starting a new life from this moment forward. I feel whole. I know myself as a true expression of Divine Love.

Spiritual Discussion

Before we met, Debbie was a very powerful healer who knew she had the assistance of Mother Mary and the angels in her healing sessions. Mother Mary was very present, assisting with our healing session from beginning to end. We could both see her Divine Light, and she was sometimes interacting with Debbie while I held sacred space. Every time Mother Mary appears, I am filled with awe and know I am so blessed to have her assistance.

In this story, Debbie spoke about her death wish that had been with her throughout her life. She had an epiphany when she realized every adopted baby must have a death wish. This is a profound spiritual truth. It is my experience almost every baby placed for adoption does have a death wish. Sometimes the death wish is conscious, and the adoptee has persistent thoughts about wishing to die. Other times the death wish is buried in the adoptee's unconscious—yet it is still there. The death wish is one of the universal soul lessons for anyone placed for adoption. Their soul wants them to discover their death wish and heal it.

Our spirit loved ones on the other side watch over us and want us to heal and complete our soul lessons. These spirits often appear in my healing sessions bringing deep soul love and the energy of forgiveness. Debbie's mother's spirit helped Debbie shift to seeing her conception with soul eyes. This was such a profound shift in consciousness for Debbie. She shifted from believing her conception was something shameful, the human point of view, to believing her conception was a perfect expression of love, the spiritual point of view.

Take note—the spirit of Debbie's mother also received a healing by participating in our session. We sometimes take our unhealed issues with us when we cross to the other side. Many times, my clients witness the spirit of a loved one receiving a healing during our session.

Guided to Earth by the Angels

I met Michelle when she was going through a midlife crisis and decided she needed some assistance. In her initial interview, she said she was married and going through the empty nest syndrome—her only daughter left for college a few years earlier. She described herself as having a life-long struggle with self-worth, anxiety, and a deep sense of unhappiness. She had tried changing careers, getting a divorce, several empty affairs, and marrying a new husband; but nothing brought relief to her inner feelings of despair.

I knew Michelle would not find an external solution to her inner state of hopelessness and despair. I explained this to Michelle saying, "You are trying to find the answer to your unhappiness by looking outside of yourself. The key to your unhappiness is held within your heart. We need to focus inside—not outside."

Intuitively, I suspected prenatal wounding of some kind. So, I said to Michelle, "Tell me about your childhood, including what you know about your birth story."

Michelle instantly confirmed my intuitive knowing! She announced, "I was adopted at birth." I felt a little blip in my heart, and I heard this message coming from Spirit, *Oh, here we go again. Another baby with prenatal wounding. It's your spiritual purpose to guide this woman on her healing journey.* I listened with a sense of excitement as Michelle shared her adoption story:

I was adopted at birth. The couple who adopted me was always open about my adoption history. From the time I can remember, I knew I was adopted. However, as a young child I didn't really know what that meant. It was just a fact to me—I didn't have any feelings about it until third grade.

Then, my third-grade teacher invited the class to play a game called "I have a secret." She directed all of us to write a secret on a piece of paper without putting a name on the paper. Then she drew out each piece of paper and had the whole class guess who had written the secret. I wrote, "I am adopted." When she read my secret, the kids in my class got very quiet. They didn't know what to say. I felt like I had done something wrong, but I didn't know what it was. I had just followed my teacher's directions and wrote down a secret. Nobody guessed it was me, so I finally told everyone, "That's my secret. I'm adopted."

The kids seemed embarrassed to know I was adopted. I felt them looking at me in a strange way—like I was different now that they knew. I suddenly felt an overwhelming shame about being adopted. For the first time, I felt like my adoption was a bad thing. Suddenly, I felt abnormal. One classmate even said to me, "Why did your parents not want you?" Of course, I had no answer. My heart hurt just thinking about it. That question was never in my thoughts before. After that shameful moment, I couldn't stop wondering, *Why? Why did they not want me?*

All of this bothered me deeply. I started shutting down. I started doing poorly in school after that day. I couldn't concentrate because I was distracted by my obsessive thoughts. *I wasn't wanted by my birth parents. I'm not really wanted here either. I have to be on guard. I have to be a really good little girl, so I won't be sent back.* Things got so bad, my parents decided I needed to repeat fourth grade, so they moved me to a different school where I could start over.

My adopted mother and my adopted grandmother always told me, "I love you." In my early years, I took those words at face value. By my teenage years, I had very negative thoughts when they told me they loved me. *They have to say that. They don't really love me.*

My adopted parents told me they tried and tried to have a baby. Finally, they gave up trying and decided to adopt. I am that adopted baby. Then surprise—my mother got pregnant just six months after my adoption. After her birth, I spent my days watching my sister become Mom's favorite. I had a front row seat watching my sister do no wrong, always the golden child. Meanwhile, I couldn't get anywhere near the two of them. I felt some invisible barrier keeping me at a great distance. So, I spent my whole childhood in a constant struggle focused on competing with my sister. Of course, I always lost. There was no way to win.

To make matters worse, this struggle was my secret. I never talked to my mother, my father, my sister, or my grandmother about my feelings related to this situation. I didn't feel safe to even begin the conversation so that left no other option than to suffer in silence. I'm 50 years old and still have not told them. Maybe I never will. My mom didn't do this on purpose. She's in denial it even happened. She's 72 years old now, and it would devastate her to hear my pain about this. I guess I think it's my issue to heal.

By the grace of God, I found my birth mother when I was 22 years old. I've always felt it was meant to be because the connection came so easily. A friend of mine overheard a conversation at a sporting event; the woman behind her on the bleachers was telling a companion about helping an adopted woman find her birth family. My friend asked if she did this for other people. The woman said yes and gave my friend her card. I called this earth angel and just five days later, I was talking on the phone to my birth mother. I was visiting my adopted parents when I made the call. My adopted mother made a video recording of that call. I was crying and laughing and jumping for joy the whole time. I still have that video. It's one of my most prized possessions.

We discovered my birth mother lived just 20 minutes from my adopted parents. She invited us to come immediately to her home. My adopted mom and I jumped in the car and raced there as fast as we could. My birth mother opened her heart and her home to both of us. She and I hugged for a very long time. I felt her love energy fill my heart as we bonded for the first time since my birth. Again, my adopted mother made a video recording of this reunion. I yearned for years and years for this to happen. My heart was full to overflowing.

My birth mother became an important part of my life. She even shared holidays with me and my adopted family. We all became one big loving blended family. It's a blessing in my life my adopted mother and my birth mother became friends. When I had my first and only baby, both my mothers immediately became loving grandmothers to my precious baby girl. Amazingly, there was no hint of competition between my two mothers. We all got along and enjoyed our feeling of deep family love. I know I am the luckiest adopted child ever.

Eventually, my birth mother also connected me to my birth father. He was much more guarded than my birth mother, so meeting him was much less emotional. I understood because I knew my birth was a secret from his wife and children for a very long time. He did say "I love you," which is what I always wanted to hear. However, he doesn't recognize me as his child. Also, he doesn't recognize my daughter as his grandchild. I'm OK with that because I don't feel like I need him. I'm just glad he didn't reject me totally. I've come to the understanding there is no right or wrong way to have a relationship with either biological parent; and it's OK for me to have different relationships with each of them.

Now I'm 50 years old so I've had this loving relationship with my birth mother for close to 30 years. She has also created a close loving relationship with my daughter, her granddaughter. In spite of that, I still think I have some unresolved issues about being adopted. I still have these feelings of anxiety, low self-esteem, and feeling unworthy. I've been to therapy, but still have not resolved these issues.

Regression Back into the Womb

Dr. Sher: Let's do a regression back into the womb. Perhaps that will help you clear your adoption issues. I've seen this work many times for others. Let yourself drift back in time and go to that time when you are a baby in the womb. As a baby in the womb you have consciousness and you have an awareness of your parents' thoughts and feelings. Your spirit is present and holds the memory of everything that happened while you were in the womb.

Michelle allowed herself to sink into a gentle state of deep relaxation. When she appeared totally relaxed, I began to ask questions of her spirit.

Dr. Sher: What are your birth mother's thoughts and feelings when she discovers she's pregnant with you?

Michelle: *Oh, shit! What am I going to do? Maybe it's not real.* Fear. Disappointment. Embarrassment. Shame. *This is not my husband's baby. What am I going to tell him? The father of my baby is a married man. He's not going to leave his family. I'm all alone in this. Abortion is not an option. I have to go through with having this baby.*

Dr. Sher: What is your birth father thinking and feeling about you being here?

Michelle: He loves my mom. My mom loves him. He can't leave his family. He regrets hurting my mom. He's sad he won't see me grow up. He's filled with a deep sadness. I feel his heartbreak. He has to keep my existence a secret. He can't let anyone know.

Dr. Sher: Now be the baby in the womb. What are you thinking and feeling?

I have this overwhelming sadness for all three of us. I feel my mom's bravery. I'm watching it and seeing it. I'm aware of my mom's feelings. I feel her deep sadness, her fear, her hopelessness about finding a way to take care of me. She's dependent on others, but they do not support keeping me.

She finds some comfort at an adoption agency. She has some peace now.

> There's a beam of light coming from my mom's womb and shining out in front of her. It's my soul light. Light is everywhere around me in the womb. I sense angels all around me. I have no fear. I'm protected.

I see light. I see a glow all around me. I'm happy in the glow. I see myself on the other side making a leap into my baby body. Angels are supporting my journey into the body. They are all around me protecting me and loving me.

I'm at the hospital being born. It's chaotic, cold, mechanical—not at all loving. I'm fighting being born. I'm not ready to leave my mother. I don't see the light anymore. I see darkness—the darkness is my emotional pain about leaving my mother. I feel like I dropped a thousand feet into the darkness. I don't want this. I want to go back into the light where I was safe.

I'm starting to see some light again. It's less than before—a little hazy. I'm alone. I'm not connected to any humans. I'm connected to the angels. I'm not all there in my body. I'm only partially there.

I see rays of light coming out of my baby body. The rays are a pale light green and some yellows that are almost white light. I see circles of light around my body. There's a very solid ring of light around me. There are beams of light coming from my body. I radiate light. I'm glowing. My own heart feels smooth and calm. I don't feel the rhythm of my mother's heart anymore, but I still feel peaceful.

I see my new parents at the foster home. My mother's mother is there with them also. I can feel my new mother's energy. She's full of happiness and lots of anxiety at the same time. She's loving and warm but also scared, very scared. My new father is there, but he stays at a distance. I can still sense him there. My new grandmother is the happiest one. She has this joy energy. She doesn't have any fear—just love and joy. She's sending me lots of love. I feel it piercing my heart. She is supporting my new mom. I feel me latching onto their energy. I'm connecting to the love energy of my new mom and my new grandmother.

These are good people. I will be OK. I sense their fear. I sense their love for me. They can't believe this is happening. They have great relief that they finally have a baby. Their prayers have been answered. I feel my connection to Heaven as I'm starting to connect to them.

Dr. Sher: You are an answer to their prayers.

Michelle: I'm the answer to somebody's prayers? Oh, my God. I never knew that. I never embraced that thought. That's amazing. Knowing that changes everything for me. I now understand I was loved through my whole journey coming to Earth. I see it. I feel it. The light is all around me again as my new mother holds me. It's as big as when I was in the womb. Angels are all around us. It's so beautiful to witness. The angels have been with me all this time!

Dr. Sher: Trust these visions are real. You've been gifted with the spiritual view of your soul journey down to Earth, your time in your mother's womb, and meeting your adopted family. Such a gift! This spiritual view is very different than the story of human pain you always believed about your birth. Trust both are real. It all depends whether you view your birth with your human eyes or your soul eyes.

Michelle: Yes. (weeping softly) These visions are a miracle! My birth is a miracle, and I'm the answer to my new mother's prayers. It was all meant to be. Now I know.

> This spiritual view of my journey to Earth changes everything. I never knew the whole journey was guided by the angels, and I was held in the Light of God.

I held sacred space and we were both silent for a very long time. There was nothing more I needed to say. I felt such joy in my heart! Once again Spirit assisted me in creating the miracle of healing for a beautiful human being who had suffered for 50 years with prenatal wounding.

One Month Later

I did a phone interview with Michelle one month after our healing session. I wanted to see how our work had influenced her life. Michelle gave me the following report:

I always believed I had a guardian angel. After our session, my connection to all my angels is more profound and so much deeper. It was one thing to believe I had one guardian angel. It's another thing to witness so many angels surrounding me. The visions Spirit showed me were so much more beautiful and grander than I ever could have imagined. I now have a sense of deep inner peace. I was so loved, and I didn't even know. I now call on all my angels. Before I thought I was all alone. For the first time, I know I was never alone.

The night of my regression I felt this overwhelming need to call my birth mother. I had some doubts about sharing all this with her, but I followed my heart. I wanted to share this spiritual view of my journey to Earth so she could also experience the miracle of healing. She listened as I shared each little detail of the visions gifted to me during the regression. I could tell she was crying as she listened. She was happy for my call. It was such a beautiful thing. This sharing was an even deeper healing for both of us. I'm so glad we could open our hearts and share my soul journey as it was revealed to me in the visions.

I've always felt like I am here for a greater purpose. At times I thought it might have something to do with helping other families heal after an adoption. However, I could never get a picture of how I would do that. The first week I was home, I was presented with an opportunity to help another family.

I have these friends who have two adopted girls. The 15-year-old wants to find her birth parents; she keeps bringing this up to her adopted parents. The adopted mother is responding with a lot of fear and resistance to letting her daughter proceed with this search. Before my regression I had a strong feeling I should intervene, but I was afraid, so I said nothing.

This week I began coaching my friends to allow their daughter to meet her birth parents. I heard myself saying to my friends, "You've got to let her meet her birth parents. Her yearning for that connection is not going to go away. Give her a chance to heal that yearning." Their fear is real. I validated that fear with understanding, but emphasized their daughter has more fear and pain about it than they will ever know. They are listening, and it's now not *if* but *when* they will support their daughter's journey and travel with her to meet her biological family.

For the future, I can see myself telling my story and sharing with others the joy of healing my adoption pain forever. My story is a gift I can share with the world.

Spiritual Discussion

One of my spiritual teachers told me years ago: "The miracle of healing happens when your client has a shift in consciousness." Michelle had numerous shifts in consciousness that happened spontaneously during and after her regression. After receiving the visions of her soul journey to Earth, Michelle shifted from "I'm all alone." to "I've always been surrounded by many angels who have protected and loved me while on the other side and after I was born here on Earth." She also shifted from, "My new family didn't really love me." to "I am the answer to their prayers, and they have always loved me." Another shift was, "I am just a human being with low self-esteem." to "I'm a spiritual being filled with Divine Light."

The most important shift for Michelle happened when she embraced the metaphysical principle her soul planned her whole journey to Earth—including that she would come through one set of parents and then be raised by a different set of parents. This shift in consciousness was very empowering for Michelle.

She expressed it this way: "I used to think of myself as a victim. I believed I was a mistake. Why me? Why did my birth parents not want me? Now I know I chose this exact journey. It was all predetermined by my soul. Switching from human logic to soul logic brought such a fundamental healing. I will never be the same."

It's important to note these shifts in consciousness are the result of emotional healing experiences that evolved during the regression session. These shifts cannot be reasoned or intellectualized in the mind. They are always the result of emotional pain being processed through the heart. This is the very essence of Radiant Heart Healing.

Michelle was 22 years old when she found her birth mother, and was received with great love. Mother and daughter even formed a wonderful loving relationship which included Michelle's adopted parents. Together they all created a big, happy blended family. In spite of all this love and connection, Michelle still carried some deep heartache about her adoption experience. Connecting with her birth mother did not clear her life-long feelings of anxiety, lack of self-worth, or her inner sense of despair.

In our phone conversation after the regression, Michelle said, "I've always wondered, why do I still have these holes? It seems these should have been healed just by finding my birth mother and feeling her love." You might also be wondering why this was so for Michelle. The answer to this question appears when we shift to a spiritual view of her adoption journey.

Michelle's reconnection with her birth mother transpired at the human level; however, it did not heal the soul loss Michelle had experienced because of her adoption. Soul loss is a disconnection from one's own soul and a disconnection from Divine Light/Love. This causes a deep searing emotional pain and cannot be healed at the human level.

Soul loss or a soul wound demands something deeper for healing. It demands a spiritual solution—a way of satisfying the deep longing for connection to one's soul and for connection to the God energy. During her regression into the womb, Michelle received the gift of spiritual healing when she was shown images of her soul light in the womb. This was a magical moment for Michelle. The next vision showed her the numerous angels who loved and protected her throughout her journey from Heaven to Earth. She was also gifted with a vision of God's light all around her as her adopted mother held her for the first time. In the moment, Michelle announced, "These visions are a miracle." Indeed, these three visions gave Michelle the spiritual healing she had been searching for her whole life. Finally, her soul loss was healed.

Love Is What Matters. It's All about Love.

Nancy arrived at my office looking a bit uneasy. I could tell she didn't know what to expect. She relaxed a bit when I gave her a big hug before we sat down to talk. I soon learned she was 66 years old and single after divorcing three times. She had one daughter and a grandson; she loved both with all her heart. Nancy also loved her career of being a hospice nurse. She knew she was called to do this work, and it fulfilled her at a very deep level. Then Nancy announced, "The main reason I'm here is to deal with my pain of being adopted. My feelings about being adopted have plagued me my whole life." Nancy also shared she had gone for therapy several times in her life but found no relief from her adoption issues.

Nancy continued:

> I don't know if you can help me. I'm here because I've felt alone, severely depressed, and unloved most of my life. As a child I was told I was adopted. The story was my birth mother had nine kids, all with the same husband. They did not keep me or any of these babies—all were placed for adoption. Then, my adopted dad's family didn't accept me. They said I was not "real family." I've always known this adoption story shaped my life. But knowing that didn't help me because I never had a clue how to fix this terrible pain I've carried my whole life.

> This adoption issue is the baggage I've carried with me everywhere I went. I could push it away sometimes. However, it was always in the corner, waiting. This woman who adopted me reinforced my belief I could be given away at any

time. At age four, she told me this story: "There are other children who live behind that bush in the front yard. If you don't behave, you will have to go live behind the bush, and they will come inside to live with me." I believed that story. I remember looking behind that bush many times to find those children. This was such a cruel thing to tell a child. Of course, I was very well behaved and did anything and everything to get my parents' approval. I spent my life pleasing everyone so I wouldn't be banished to behind the bush.

Thank God, I did find some love in my adopted family. My mother's father lived with us, and he adored me. He was my rock. I was devastated at 7 years old when he died. In addition, my mother's sister, her husband, and son Michael lived in our home. They also gave me a lot of love. Michael and I were the same age and we had so much fun together. They moved out when I was 6 years old. Looking back, these kind relatives in my adopted family saved my life—they gave me love.

I've been married three times, and all my marriages were failures. I married right out of high school and divorced within a few months. We were both just too young and never should have married. My second marriage lasted nine miserable years. He was addicted to alcohol and gambling, and I finally got the courage to leave. My third husband was also an addict who drank and used pot and other drugs. I never felt loved by any of these men. The one blessing is I got my daughter from the third marriage. I've loved her from the time I knew I was pregnant. She is the love of my life.

I explained to Nancy she had an unconscious belief: *I am not lovable.* Because of this belief, she sent out a vibration which attracted men who were very wounded emotionally and could not be loving. Nancy seemed to have a defining moment as she took in this information about attracting unloving men. Knowing Nancy was placed for adoption, I intuitively knew this destructive belief was the result of being emotionally wounded while in the womb. I explained to Nancy we could do a gentle regression back into the womb and observe what happened during that time. Nancy immediately agreed to do the regression.

Regression Back into the Womb

Dr. Sher: What's your mother's first thought when she discovers she is pregnant with you? What is she feeling?

Nancy: I hear her thinking. *Oh, no. Not again. I don't want it to be here. I just have to abort this baby. I don't have the courage. If I don't do any prenatal care maybe, I'll have a miscarriage. This baby is a big inconvenience. I'm terrified to tell my husband. What will he say or do? He's going to be so angry. I'm so afraid of him. He's abusive already and he's going to get worse.*

Dr. Sher: Imagine your mother telling your father, "I'm pregnant. We are going to have another baby." What is he thinking and feeling?

Nancy: My father is so angry. He's filled with rage. He tells her, "It's all your fault. Who's going to take this one?" I see him raising his hand to hit her. He beats her really bad. He's hoping to end the pregnancy if he hits her hard enough. From within the womb, I can hear him raging, and I feel his rage. I'm really scared. My mother is filled with fear also.

Dr. Sher: Now be the baby in the womb. What are you experiencing?

Nancy was quiet for a few moments and then she said:

There's a very heavy energy in the womb. There's this deep grief all around me. It's very depressing. My mother's womb is filled with pain. It's so uncomfortable for me. Feeling it now takes my breath away. My mother doesn't talk to me. There's no connection. She just wants it to be over. This heavy energy is very scary. I'm filled with fear—fear fills all my baby cells. I'm afraid she might do something to make an abortion happen.

I can hear myself thinking. *I want to be born. I want to be out of this toxic womb. I want to escape the pain. I'm not safe in this womb. I'm defective. I'm not worth anything. I'm not worth loving. I can't trust myself or other people. The world is not a good or safe place to be.*

Now I see a little glimmer of light in all the pain. Oh, my God! There's an angel in the womb with me. She says her name is Ann. She says she's been with me all along. She's my guardian angel. She has been there right from the beginning, but I didn't know. Ann has always loved me and has been keeping me safe. She has looked after me and cared for me my whole life. She has been waiting for me to wake up and know she is with me now and has been from the beginning. She's laughing and she says, "It's about time!" This is so amazing. I didn't know. I just didn't know.

Now I see myself being delivered at the hospital. The whole birthing process is very mechanical. There is no love from my mother—she doesn't even hold me or look at me. My biological father is not even present. They don't even care who takes me home from the hospital. What's wrong with me? There has to be something wrong with me that they let me be taken away like trash.

I'm so angry! They didn't even bother to look at me or know me. They don't care if anyone is going to adopt me or not. I can't stop talking. I'm filled with grief watching this hospital scene. And… I'm filled with fear. My whole body is shaking with fear. Will anyone even adopt me?

Dr. Sher: Keep sobbing. Keep releasing. It's time you release all this pain, fear and anger you've carried your whole life.

I was quiet as I deliberately created a protected space for Nancy so she could release her deep grief, anger, and terror about her birth experience. She wept from the very depths of her being. She wept like she would never stop. I put my arms around Nancy and held her like a little child until her sobbing dissipated. It took a long time, but eventually Nancy found a place of peace beneath her emotional pain.

Suddenly, without my guidance, Nancy was enveloped with the energy of Divine Light/Love all around her. The Divine Light filled the whole room. She saw Ann, her guardian angel surrounding her in the Light of God. The light was incredible. It was so bright; we both could see it and feel it. It was something to behold! Such an awesome moment! We both sat in absolute silence—neither one of us wanting to disturb this mystical moment created by Spirit. Then Nancy was given a vision of herself as the baby in the womb laughing and doing flips while her guardian angel watched over her, keeping her safe. Nancy burst into laughter as she described this vision brought by Spirit. This was such a gift!

Next, I guided Nancy on a spiritual journey. I invited her to see her spirit-self lying on her back on a pink cloud. The energy of unconditional love wrapped all around her, so she felt very safe. Then I suggested the pink cloud could lift her up into the light so she could have a visit to the other side. Nancy reported these visions given to her by Spirit:

I see people all around me. I know some of them, and I'm so happy to see them. There's my daughter and my grandson and some dear friends. They all have a light shining from within. They're all radiant. A voice is telling me, *This is your tribe.* I feel filled with so much love as I see these beings and know I belong with them.

Now my cousin Mike from my adopted family is emerging from the distance. We were always close. He was murdered at age 24. It's still an unsolved case. He's telling me he knew he wouldn't be here long—that was the plan. He was happy in the years he had here on Earth. He always felt my love.

Mike gives me a message. *I've been watching over you. I'm so happy you found your guardian angel named Ann. I'm so happy you released all that pain. I'm proud of you. You need to know you are loved.* He's sending me a gold beam of love. It has a deep red center. He sends me a big red valentine and places it right in my heart. He has so much love for me. I'm overwhelmed with all his love. I can feel it filling my whole chest. Now, he says:

> *Don't hold on to the pain of your adoption.*
> *Let it go. Love is what matters. It's all about love.*

Changes for Nancy after Our Healing Session

I did a phone interview with Nancy several months after her healing session. Here are the changes she reported after our regression:

My regression back into the womb had a profound effect on me. I feel so different. The best thing is I no longer feel defective. That is such a miracle! I've always thought there was something wrong with me. It's amazing to me a belief I've held my whole life could just dissolve in one session.

I also know I am supposed to be here. This is so new for me. I released all my emotional pain about my adoption. All those old hurts and negative beliefs about myself are just gone. I never met my birth parents or any of my siblings. It just doesn't matter anymore. I now understand everything unfolded exactly as my soul planned. I am finally at peace about my birth.

I have let go of constantly competing with others. I find I no longer need to seek the approval of others. In addition, I have more confidence in my decisions. These three shifts are huge for me! Three life-long negative patterns are no longer a part of me. These changes happened without me even thinking about them. I woke up one day and simply observed I was thinking and behaving in a whole new way. I am so grateful.

I feel Ann, my guardian angel, around me and guiding me through life. When I need guidance about a decision, I start praying and immediately sense her presence. Sometimes I hear her speaking to me also. It's so comforting to know she's watching over me. I never feel alone anymore. This is such a blessing after feeling so alone my whole life.

Seeing myself, my daughter, my grandson, and my friends as Radiant Beings in the Light of God is a scene etched in my heart for eternity. It was so glorious to recognize their spirit energy. I know them at the soul level. I feel so happy every time I remember the vision. It was so healing to hear that spirit voice say, *This is your tribe.* I've felt so alone my whole life. Not anymore. Whenever I recall the voice and my people in the light, I know I belong. This is my family of the heart. I cherish that feeling of belonging to my tribe. We are connected in love—and that's more important than being connected through blood.

After my healing session with you, my cousin Mike has continued to come for visitations. This is all new to me; I couldn't reach him before our session. For some time, I've been dealing with issues that have surfaced about my adopted mother. I could not feel forgiveness, and at first, I thought it was OK. Then Mike came to me again, and encouraged me to forgive because it is no longer about her; the forgiveness is for me. He explained forgiveness doesn't mean what happened is all right. He told me to let the anger go and move forward in love. The messages he brings me always end with, "Love is all that matters."

It haunts me the person who murdered Mike has never been found. One day as I was driving down the road and thinking about the murder, I could feel Mike's presence in the car with me. He was not in his physical form but more of a divine spiritual form. He was a mass of golden light in the passenger seat of my car. I could hear him talking to me in my head.

Mike told me forgiveness is important to move forward. I asked if he had forgiveness for the person who took his life, and he told me yes. I said if I knew who did this, then maybe I could get to forgiveness, too. Then Mike sent me another interesting message. *Having that information is not important and will not change anything. I will still be where I am. Knowing who did this will not bring any closure at all for you. I will still be gone from the physical world. Then he told me very clearly:*

> *Love is forgiveness and love is all there is.*
> *It's all that matters.*

My cousin Mike's profound words are still resonating within me. *Don't hold on to the pain of your adoption. Let it go. Love is what matters. It's all about love.* I am truly focused on the love—Mike's love flowing into me from the other side, the soul love shared within my tribe, the spiritual love from Ann, my guardian angel, the love I share with my hospice patients, and the love I share with my daughter and grandson. My life is all about love.

Spiritual Discussion

This story demonstrates Nancy is a very courageous soul who created a very difficult soul plan. Her soul chose to be born to cold-hearted, unloving parents who had no room in their hearts for a baby. Her soul plan also included being adopted by another cold-hearted mother who threatened to banish Nancy to behind the bush if she didn't behave. Her deep emotional pain of feeling defective, alone, and unloved pushed her to find a way to heal her deep soul wound.

Nancy's soul plan also included three important people from her adopted family: her maternal grandfather, her mother's sister, and her cousin Michael. These three souls gave Nancy the only love she had as a child. I can imagine all of these souls on the other side making an agreement with Nancy's soul that they would be present in her early childhood to share love with her and bring some joy into her life.

This story, like Debbie's story earlier in this chapter, shows us once again, the spirit of a loved one can appear and assist with a client's healing. Nancy's adopted cousin, Michael, gave her such a healing message: *Love is what matters. It's all about love.* Notice he simply appeared without being called. Neither Nancy nor I would have thought to call him. I know intuitively their soul plan contained an agreement that Michael would continue loving and assisting Nancy from the other side.

As we have seen in many other stories: **Love is the most powerful healing force on the planet.** In this case, it is not a mother's love that brings the healing for Nancy. It's the high frequency of Divine Love from her guardian angel who appears in the womb, and the spirit of her cousin Michael who sends her a message of soul love from the other side. I trust Nancy will move forward in life, enjoying her soul growth, and always remembering her soul lessons that emerged during the regression. *Let go of the pain. Love is what matters. It's all about love.*

My Mother Loves Me. I Can Feel It!

I first heard about Lily from her adopted mother, Joan, who is a very wonderful loving woman. Joan came into my life when she attended one of my workshops on Radiant Heart Healing in East Lansing, Michigan. She had explored spiritual matters for years through reading books and attending spiritual workshops. She felt guided to come to my workshop, but she didn't really know why she was there. As I talked about the unwanted-unloved baby syndrome, Joan suddenly understood she was guided to come so she could heal her prenatal trauma. She also understood she was guided to be there for another very important purpose. She *got it* immediately how Lily, her 11-year-old adopted daughter, must have prenatal wounding.

Joan is very metaphysical, laughs easily, and has a wonderful open way about her. Joan and Lily have a great mother-daughter relationship, and they are also best friends. They talk about feelings and have rather deep spiritual conversations. Consequently, Lily is very mature for her age and very aware of herself and the world around her. Talking to Lily was like talking to a very wise adult who just happens to be in a preteen body.

Joan scheduled a private healing session with me immediately after the workshop. She was able to release the deep pain of her prenatal wounding and fill up with the energy of Divine Light/ Love. Even though she was married and had created a very loving family, this was the first time Joan felt like she opened her heart to receive love. She was amazed by this experience! She was so deeply moved, she decided to share this experience with her daughter. Lily listened to her mother as she described her healing session and immediately announced, "I want my own session with that lady."

Joan reported to me, "The power of that statement got me moving. I've learned Lily knows what she needs, and I trusted that in this case. So, I called you the same night and asked you to work with my daughter. When you said you didn't do kids, I persisted. I don't know what I said that changed your mind, but you suddenly switched your position and agreed to see Lily."

Lily is a precocious African American girl, and her adopted mother is white. It was a bit of a shock when I first saw them together. Joan didn't even think to tell me. At first glance, Lily appeared to be a typical budding preteen wearing jeans and listening to pop music through her headphones. She loves talking on the phone for hours, imitates the dancers on YouTube, and often changes her clothes four times before being satisfied with her appearance for school. Her adopted mother Joan described her as massively adolescent. Lily is definitely adolescent, but believe me, she is anything but typical!

Lily's story is included in this book because she had prenatal wounding after being placed for adoption. She had been dealing with grief about missing her birth mother ever since she could remember. Lily was placed for adoption just two days after birth, and she had this intense yearning to find her birth mother. Her adopted mother Joan gave this description of Lily's heartache:

> Lily has been in pain about her birth mother from the time she could understand about adoption. She talks about her of-

ten and has this intensity about finding her. She's angry that the adoption laws restrict her from even looking for her birth mother until she is 18. For whatever reason, she has no pain about her birth father and no interest in finding him. I find that very curious.

Lily cries a lot about missing her birth mother. Any time she thinks about her, she starts to cry. Sometimes we are driving, and she starts crying so hard I have to stop the car and spend time holding her until she is all cried out.

I feel so helpless when she goes into her pain about this. There's no solution. There's nothing I can do. My own heart aches just holding her and listening to her grief. Luckily, Lily isn't always in that terrible pain. She does these intense releases, and then she gets on with her everyday busy life—until the next time.

This story is about Lily healing her grief regarding her birth mother. She found her way to me because at the human level she had the guidance of her adopted mother, Joan. I also believe this whole story was guided by Spirit because it unfolded effortlessly, as if by some divine plan. It certainly wasn't something I planned because I've said for years I only work with adults. When Joan first asked me to work with Lily I answered, "I don't think so. I don't do kids." And yet two weeks later, I found myself working with this 11-year-old child on a cold February day in East Lansing, Michigan.

The Adoption Selection Process

Lily's soul plan also included having a sensitive, loving adopted father. Lily's birth parents were both African American, and yet her birth mother chose a white couple to adopt Lily. Joan and her husband Richard were the chosen ones. Joan explained how this came to be:

> The adoption agency asked us to write our autobiographies and a letter about why we wanted to adopt a child. Lily's birth mother was then given this information about several potential adopting families. She chose us, knowing we were a white couple. Her major reason for choosing us was she wanted a stable couple so Lily could have both a mother and a father.

Lily's birth mother had a lot of pain about not having a father in her life, so she wanted Lily to have a father. The story is she was also adopted, and her adopted mother was a single African American teacher. This woman was very upset when her adopted daughter chose a white family for Lily. Lily's birth mother overcame these objections and held to her conviction that Joan and Richard were the right family for Lily.

Richard is a very sensitive man, and he has imparted that to Lily. Joan told me this story to illustrate his sensitive nature:

> We knew we were selected as the adopted parents for an African American baby girl. While driving to meet her for the first time, Richard and I were having this discussion about the baby's name. At some point I suggested using his mother's name, Lily. He was so touched by this that he burst into tears. After that there was no question; she had to be Lily.

Richard was educated as a biochemist, but he left that career to follow his dreams and create a music store. He's a musician himself, and through the store he sells musical instruments and provides music lessons for children. The store has been a huge success for 30 years.

Lily has an incredible gift for singing, so her adopted father's interest in music has been a wonderful bonding experience for the two of them. He supports her taking lessons in dance, singing, music, and all the creative arts. She's a natural at both dancing and singing. Lily tried out for the Michigan State University Children's Choir and made it. She's one of 65 children who travel and compete in choral competitions.

Lily's father says he's not spiritual; however, I know he is because he has such a loving heart, and he expresses his spirituality through his music. He is also the eternal optimist. He knows thoughts are energy and very much believes in the importance of positive thoughts. Consequently, he never worries. Richard has an open mind about Joan taking Lily to psychic readings and healing sessions. Joan says, "Richard says he doesn't believe in all this spiritual stuff, but he doesn't get in the way."

Maya, Lily's Guardian Angel

Lily's soul plan also included having a guardian angel, Maya. It's an interesting story about how Lily met Maya. Joan took Lily to a spiritual reader who sits with people and does a drawing of their guides or angels. Lily was only ten years old at the time, and she was thrilled to accompany her mother for this session. As Lily sat for her own session, the artist drew a picture of a beautiful angel. Lily fell in love with this angel and spontaneously named her Maya. This choice was quite profound because Maya is a major African Goddess of Creation. Lily had no way of consciously knowing this at the time; yet, she picked this name. Amazing child! Lily loves her angel drawing and has it hanging at the head of her bed. She does a little ritual every night and says her prayers to Maya. Obviously, the idea of a guardian angel provides Lily with a sense of protection and safety.

Lily's Healing Session

I decided to work with Lily just like I would work with an adult client. So, I briefly explained the Radiant Heart Healing process to her, and we began. Immediately, I sensed Lily was very powerful at using visualizations and very sensitive to energy. She could feel the Earth energy moving through her body and coming into her heart. She could see the bright light of spiritual love energy and actually describe it to me. From the very beginning, I knew this was going to be a truly special healing session. This child was an incredibly powerful little being! She was only little in her physical body—she had a great powerful spirit.

Using gentle relaxation techniques, I guided Lily back into the womb. Her instructions were to answer these questions with the first thing that came into her mind.

Dr. Sher: I want you to go to the moment of discovery. That's the moment when your birth mother first figures out she's pregnant with you. What is her first thought?

Lily: *Oh, my gosh!*

Dr. Sher: What is she feeling?

Lily: Discombobulated. Confused. She's very scared.

Dr. Sher: Now go to the moment when she tells your birth father she's pregnant. What is his first thought?

Lily looked stricken with fear and I could feel her whole body tighten. She closed down her energy and put up a shield. I could actually feel her withdrawing into herself.

Lily: (whispering and shaking her head) I can't say.

Dr. Sher: Can I tell you what I heard?

Lily: (Says nothing, but she nods her head yes.)

Dr. Sher: He said, "Let's get rid of her."

Lily: No, he said, "Let's get rid of it!"

Dr. Sher: It's true, Lily. You can trust what you heard. He wants your mother to get an abortion. You've always known this on some level, haven't you?

Lily: Yes.

Sher: Let's see what happens next. What is your father feeling?

Lily: Anger. No, it's rage. He swears a lot. My mom is afraid of him.

We were both quiet for a time. I started seeing many scenes unfolding, one after another, in my mind's eye. These were nothing I ever would have created. It was as if Spirit started showing me a video of scenes with Lily's birth parents. They were in a heated argument. I saw Lily's birth father shove her mother against the wall. Then he bashed her head numerous times.

Lily was very quiet while I was getting these images. I didn't know what was happening in her inner mind, but I could tell she seemed very tense. I decided not to share these scenes with her so as not to frighten her.

Dr. Sher: Are you hearing something or seeing something in your mind?

Lily: He hits my mom. He pushes her against the wall and he's hitting her head.

Dr. Sher: Yes, it's true, Lily. I'm getting the same images. What happens next?

Lily: Mom says, "Let's get out of here. Don't worry. I'll take care of you." I think she's talking to me in her tummy.

Dr. Sher: Yes, Lily. I'm getting the same message. Now I want you to be the baby. Be yourself and tell me, what are you thinking about yourself?

Lily: (long pause) I want to see what's going to happen.

Dr. Sher: Do you have any thoughts about going back to the light?

Lily: Oh, no! I want to go forward.

Dr. Sher: You have such a strong life wish! Good for you! What happens next?

Lily: We go to the hospital so I can get born. It's very painful getting born. My body hurts all over. I'm being squeezed very hard.

Spirit is showing both of us a video with the same scenes about Lily's birth. I'm watching this scene in a typical hospital delivery room as Lily is talking about being squeezed. Then I see this luminescent spiritual light flood the whole room. This incredible Divine Light appears at the very second Lily slips from her mother's body and is delivered into the hands of the male doctor.

Lily: Maya is here! She's right there next to me as I'm being born. I can see her! She looks just the same as the picture over my bed.

Dr. Sher: I see her light. She lights up the whole room, doesn't she?

Lily: (smiling and laughing) Yes, she's so amazing; she lights up the whole room.

Dr. Sher: What happens next?

Lily: The nurses wrap me up and give me to my birth mom. She holds me a long time. She keeps looking at me and smiling.

> I can feel my mother's heart. She loves me! I can feel it.
> I never knew. This changes everything.

Lily had this look of incredible joy on her face as she felt her birth mother's love. Her aura got very bright and expansive. She was all lit up. We sat there for some time with Lily connecting to her mother's heart. Every few seconds she kept repeating: "My mother loves me. I can feel it."

Dr. Sher: Yes, Lily. Your mother loves you. Trust this is real. You can feel it, and I feel it too.

Lily: Now I see they are taking me away to another place. Maya comes with me. I'm in a real little bed. Maya stands by the bed. She just stands there and lights up the whole room. I keep saying, "Where's my mom? Where's my mom?" I'm feeling lots of hurt in my heart. I want my mom, but nobody hears me. Nobody takes me back to my mom. I don't know where she is.

Lily was saying all of this very slowly as the scene unfolded in her mind. I'm tuning in to the same scene, and there is this luminescent light glowing in the nursery. As Lily talked about the hurt in her heart, I connected to that and felt this excruciating pain in my own heart. The grief was unbearable! The words that came to me were, "They are ripping my heart out."

Dr. Sher: Lily, you have carried this hurt in your heart your whole life. It's not good to keep the hurt. Let me help you let go of the hurt and keep Mom's love. Are you willing to do that?

Lily: OK.

Dr. Sher: Ask Spirit to show you a color that represents this hurt in your heart.

Lily: It's a muddy purple.

Dr. Sher: Good. Now scan your body and tell me where you see it. I'll scan too, and we can compare notes.

Lily: (pause) There's a lot in my heart, but it's everywhere, too.

Dr. Sher: That's right. The hurt is in every cell of your body. So, I want you to visualize the muddy purple energy leaving every cell, flowing through your body into your chest cavity, and forming a big ball. I can feel what's happening with the energy, so I'll guide you as you do it.

My body becomes like a biofeedback machine when I'm working like this with clients. I feel all the energy movements the person feels. I also get an awareness about what is happening with the energy. As we did this visualization, I could sense the muddy purple energy moving very quickly through Lily's body. In just a few minutes, she amassed this huge ball of hurt energy in her chest cavity. In fact, the ball was so big it expanded way out in front of her chest. I took my hand and felt for the edge of the ball. It extended a full 12 inches out in front of her physical body. I was so intrigued with the size of the ball, I had Lily open her eyes and see where my hand was. We sat there looking at each other in utter amazement! So much hurt!

Then I guided Lily through a simple visualization to release all the hurt. We imagined the muddy purple ball becoming a balloon. Lily opened the balloon with her mind and then saw this purple geyser of energy gushing out of the center of her chest. She could see it, and I could feel it with my hand. It was something to behold. This geyser of very hot energy poured out of her chest hitting against my hand. It continued for almost five minutes.

Dr. Sher: I felt the vibration change. Did the geyser change colors?

Lily: Yes, now it's a rose color.

Dr. Sher: That's good. Keep sending it out with your mind. Now keep watching the colors. It changed again, didn't it?

Lily: Yes, now it's a lighter rose.

Dr. Sher: Good. Keep watching what it does.

Lily: It went to all white.

Dr. Sher: Yes, I felt it. That means we cleared all the hurt energy.

Lily: The colors have music. Did you hear the music?

Lily was very matter of fact when she announced this. She *knew* because she could hear the music. She didn't hear it with her physical ears but, rather, with her spiritual ears. She trusted her perception just the same. Lily is very used to tuning in to the higher vibrations and perceiving sounds and sights beyond her ordinary five-sense reality.

Dr. Sher: No. I can't hear it, but I believe you. My spiritual colleagues tell me the colors always have music on the other side. I'm amazed you can hear it.

Lily: It's really cool. (laughing) Wow! Colors with music!

Dr. Sher: (laughing) Lily, you are just something else! I just love working with you!

Lily: Yeah, this is fun. And it's so easy.

Dr. Sher: We're almost done. I can tell you are getting restless, but we have just a few more minutes. We need to fill the hurt places with healing energy. Imagine this big ball of very shiny energy. It's sparkling light, like when the sun shines on the water. See that kind of light coming in the top of your head and coming down filling your chest cavity. Let's make a huge ball of this healing energy in your chest. Good, you're doing it. Can you feel that?

Lily: Yes, my chest is getting real hot, and it feels real full.

Dr. Sher: That's it. Your heart is full of Divine Light/Love. That sparkling light is God's Love. This is God's love flowing into your chest. Imagine the light going into every cell of your body. As the light fills your whole body, I want you to take in these messages:

You are a beautiful child of God. You are a gift to the world.

Your birth was not an accident. You were born at the exact right time for you.

Your soul knew, coming in, you would leave your birth mom and find Joan and her husband Richard. This was all meant to be.

Everything is unfolding exactly according to plan. Your angel Maya has always been with you. Maya is here to love you and protect you.

You are surrounded with love. God loves you. Your birth mother loves you. Joan loves you. Richard loves you. You deserve to open your heart and feel all this love.

As we finished, Lily and I shared a long hug, and then she reverted to her adolescent pastime of listening to her favorite music using her headphones. Joan and I sat talking about the session while Lily danced to her favorite music and tuned us out completely. Funny how one minute she was this spiritually evolved being, and the next minute she was just an ordinary preteen. Lily seemed to switch easily from one to the other.

Changes for Lily

I interviewed Lily on the phone four months after our prenatal healing. I asked her to describe how she had changed since our session. She replied:

> I feel very quiet inside. I'm more comfortable with being adopted. I have more understanding about why my birth mother had to give me up. I also understand why I never wanted to meet my birth father. At this point I would not want to be living with my birth mother. But I still want to find her when I'm 18.

I also asked Joan to describe any changes in Lily since our healing session. Joan said:

> Lily's pain about her birth mother is totally gone. This is a huge relief to Lily as well as her father and me. We both felt so helpless when she had those bouts of grief. She has not cried once about her birth mother in the past four months. It's over.

> Lily talks about her birth mother a lot less. It's been a big lack in her life. Now she no longer has to wonder if her mother loved her. Lily knows for certain she did. This has made all the difference in the world. I think this knowing filled the aching hole in Lily's heart. Lily told her adopted father, Richard, she

still intends to search for her birth mother when she is 18. Lily said to him, "Even if I find her in a cemetery, I'll feel much better knowing where she is."

It's been four months since Lily's time with you. She still has a vivid memory of all the details in her session. She accepts the scenes that came to her as the absolute truth about her birth. She has no doubting thoughts like, "I must have imagined all this."

Spiritual Discussion

The key moment in this session is when Lily discovers her birth mother's love. During the regression, she actually feels it with every fiber of her being. Even her aura brightens and gets bigger. This is the most significant healing moment for this adopted child. Her words are: "I can feel her heart. She loves me!" Lily's deep soul wound of being separated from her mother is healed in an instant. Joan reports Lily no longer yearns for her birth mother—her grief about losing her birth mother is healed. Lily comes to a sense of spiritual peace about her adoption. And so, we see once again: **Love is the most powerful healing force in the Universe.**

Adoption is not a mistake, an accident, or a chance occurrence—rather it is part of the baby's soul plan. At the human level, people are not aware of the plan they each developed before coming to Earth. In both conception and adoption there are no accidents. From the spiritual perspective, the adoption process is one of ancient promises being kept. These promises were made between the souls of the baby, the birth mother, the birth father, the adopted mother, and the adopted father. Then all these promises are forgotten when these souls come to Earth because the veil of forgetfulness envelopes their consciousness and blocks all memory of these previous agreements.

Most people have an energy block between our human world and the Spirit World. This block is sometimes called *the veil of forgetfulness* or just *the veil*. This veil prevents us from remembering our existence before being born into this current life. When the veil is in place, the person has no conscious memory of any past life experiences, being a soul on the other side, or creating a soul plan for this lifetime. People on a path of spiritual evolution often have a goal to pierce or lift the veil and be able to see into the Spirit World where our angels, archangels, master teachers, spirit guides, and loved ones now reside. Regressing back into the womb is one way of piercing the veil that blocks our memory of our time in the womb.

Each soul makes a choice to come to Earth. The very purpose of the soul journey here on Earth is to learn lessons and achieve soul growth by accomplishing the tasks the soul chose before coming. The soul lessons for any baby placed for adoption include experiencing the deep pain of separation from the birth mother, releasing the pain, and then healing the heartache by feeling the birth mother's deep love during a regression experience. Receiving the energy of Divine Love during a regression session can also heal the pain of adoption. It is clear Lily completed her soul lessons about her adoption. How wonderful she could accomplish this at age 11. Her suffering about this issue is finished, and she can move forward in life, feeling spiritual peace and Divine Love.

You might be carrying the heartache and emotional pain of being adopted. My hope for you is that you heal your soul wound as early as possible. You deserve to be free of suffering and fill your life with peace, joy, and love.

I Am Conscious in the Womb

Marla is a licensed acupuncturist as well as a psychic/medium, and a spiritual healer who does energy healing in Sedona, Arizona. Before coming to Sedona, she spent 20 plus years seeing 15 to 20 patients a day in her private practice in California. At that time, her practice was focused on pain relief and healing physical issues. Now she still does acupuncture, but her focus has changed to helping her clients awaken spiritually and evolve to higher levels of consciousness.

Marla lives a life focused on her spiritual purpose of bringing more Divine Light to the world. She lives a holistic lifestyle that includes being in meditation 1 to 4 hours a day. She is also the mother of two adult children and the grandmother of a little girl she simply adores. When in her presence, I can feel she is grounded with an open, loving heart filled with compassion for those suffering in the world. She also has a sense of deep spiritual peace and a loving heart light that shines out to the world.

Marla was born to an unwed mother in 1954 in Michigan and placed by private adoption with a very loving rural family in Iowa. At that time, it was very rare for an unwed mother to keep her baby. Marla felt very loved in her new family which included two adopted brothers who were seven years older. They both adored her and took her everywhere with them. Marla grew up knowing she was adopted but had no longing to meet her birth parents. She felt totally loved within her adopted family and was happy and content where she was.

It was not an easy childhood for several reasons. First, they were a very poor rural family. Second, her adopted dad had times when he really lost his temper, so the kids were fearful of him and learned to stay out of his way. Third, her mom was always in poor health because of diabetes; she died when Marla was only 11 years old. None of these experiences seemed to impact Marla very much. She believes she learned important soul lessons dealing with each of these circumstances.

Marla reported she never felt poor because her adopted parents knew how to stretch a dime into a dollar. They had the basics of a roof over their head, food they raised on their little farm, and a home filled with love. In spite of his rage, her adopted dad was devoted to the children and did things like teach Sunday School, be a Boy Scout Leader, and take the family on vacations. Her adopted mom protected the kids and devoted herself to giving her three adopted children the best life she could provide. She even ironed sheets for 10 cents an hour so she could give Marla dance lessons and keep all three children in sports. She loved being a mother, and the kids all felt her profound mother love.

Marla had no heartache about being placed for adoption and no yearning to know about her birth parents. She had no resentments towards her birth mother. She knew it was all meant to be. Marla's adopted mother always told her:

> "It takes more love to give up a child than
> to raise that child in a bad situation."

After her adopted mother's transition, Marla continued to live with her father and spent most of her time out of the house. She did a lot of baby sitting and spent her free time in the homes of her close girlfriends. Marla continued as before and learned to compartmentalize her grief. As a teen she remembers putting all the icky things in a box. It was her way of coping, and it worked for a long time. She didn't even cry until years later.

Description of Time in the Womb

I regressed Marla back into the womb. Since she meditates so much, it was very easy for her to access her womb experience. Marla gave me this description:

> I'm in the womb. There's no light. It's warm and very fluid. I have this sense of floating; it's very nice. I like it. I'm comfortable. My birth mom doesn't know she's pregnant.

I'm conscious. I'm totally connected to the Spirit World. I'm feeling *at one* with Spirit. There is no veil between my consciousness and Spirit. I'm as conscious then as I am right now at the age of 65.

> I already know I'm going to be given up. It was
> an agreement I made before coming here.
> I was part of that agreement.

I've been in the womb for three months now. My birth mother has discovered she's pregnant. She's very emotional—filled with fear. She has lots of fear about telling her parents. She's only 19 years old. She tells her mother, but not her father. Her emotions are not affecting me. I have this protective grid around me. It was placed there by Spirit. It's all the colors of the rainbow. It protects me from her negative emotions.

I'm conscious I've chosen this other family. So, I'm happy and content knowing I will be raised by them. I'm aware I chose this birth route. I was supposed to come through my birth mom, but I know I'm not hers. She is only a surrogate for my true mother—the mother my soul has chosen. My true mother can't birth a child so coming through my birth mother is the only way to get to my true mother.

Now I'm at eight months in the womb. My birth mother is crying about having to give me up. She has thoughts of keeping me with her. Her crying does not affect me at all. I still have this rainbow energy all around me in the womb. She is very distraught. I'm protected from her negative emotions. I'm very blissful and happy. She doesn't have any thoughts about abortion.

I don't know if I'm a boy or a girl while in the womb. It's not important to me. I know my purpose here, but it doesn't matter whether I'm male or female. I'm conscious and connected to Spirit. I know what I'm here to do. I'm here to serve humanity through healing and helping others. I know I've chosen the new family I'm going to. I know all this in the womb because there is no veil. When the veil comes over us, we forget our soul plan. We are no longer conscious.

My birth mother goes to live with my new family for the last three months of the pregnancy. She has lots of doubts about giving me up to them. She's from a wealthy family, and my new family is very poor. She's worried they won't take good care of me. She's only 19, and my new parents are both 31 years old. She is crying a lot these months before I'm born. Lots of drama. I still have the rainbow energy all around me, so I'm still protected from her emotions.

My birth mother has huge fears about labor and delivery. My adopted parents take her to the hospital. The doctors sedate her. I'm delivered rather easily. My birth mother got to see me and hold me. I have lots of dark hair.

Then I'm taken to be with my new family out in the hallway. They give me to my new father first. He holds me for a short time. Then they give me to my new mother. She is thrilled I'm a girl. They already have two adopted boys. I know my true mother is thinking, *Our family is complete now.*

I have lots of love in my new family. I'm the golden child. My two brothers adore me, and they hold me a lot. My clothes are not comfortable. My mother likes to play dress up with me. I'm in girly chiffon dresses that are scratchy.

I'm aware of past lives with my chosen mother. We've been in close family relationships in other lifetimes. I see we were sisters at one time. I come into this lifetime with the full knowledge she will cross over early. It is all pre-written—my whole life journey and all that will unfold. I don't see previous lives with my dad or my brothers. This past life connection is only with my chosen mom.

I'm moving forward in time. I'm 2 years old, and I know I can breathe under water. This is a past life memory. Every time I take a bath, I try to suck the oxygen out of the water. I'm driving my new mother crazy trying again and again and again. I'm obsessed. I won't give up. I try hundreds of times. I have a strong memory of knowing how to do this. I don't understand why I can't do it now. I try to get oxygen out of the water from ages two to six. It is very annoying. I get so frustrated when I can't do it.

I have a memory of a past life in Atlantis. There I could breathe under water. I was always loving the water. I was more comfortable in the water than on land. As a child in this lifetime I also love the water. My mother could not swim, but my brothers took me out in the lake when I was six months old. From then on, I was in the water all the time. To this day, I love the water. I love to swim.

When we finished the regression, Marla and I were both quiet for a very long time. She seemed to be in a state of quiet reflection—pondering all she had experienced as a baby in the womb. It was a lot to take in. Then she said:

This regression revealed some fascinating information about my time in the womb. I've never done a regression before, so I didn't know what to expect. Since I meditate so much, it was very easy for me to become the baby in the womb. I was pleasantly surprised to find I was conscious in the womb. Until this regression, I had no awareness of that, and no awareness of my soul plan to come through one mother and go to another family. When the veil came down at age three, all that knowledge must have gone into my unconscious memory and was stored there till we accessed it just now.

My chosen mother was not conscious during her life with me here on Earth. She accepted I was a very unusual, sensitive child. However, she had no idea I was a conscious being while in the womb. She loved being my mother. I was such a joy to her. She's been in spirit for 54 years now. At this time, she is very evolved spiritually—she grew on the other side. She's a guardian angel for me, my children, and my grandchild.

When I was 11 years old, my chosen mother's death brought me to a very deep place spiritually. The only thing I had was gone. My brothers had joined the military by that time. I wanted to stay away from my father's unpredictable rages. So, my whole thing was God. I had a loneliness in my soul. Somehow, I knew I was missing my connection with Source. I went to church a lot to pray. Actually, I went every day for years. During prayer, my loneliness was replaced with a deep spiritual peace and a feeling of oneness with Spirit. This soothed my soul. In my early teens, I formed a one to one relationship with God. I'm blessed to have that relationship to this day.

Hearing Marla describe her early relationship with God and a feeling of oneness with Spirit, helped me understand this woman's life path to become a healer. I felt honored to know about this part of her early life. Marla continued to share more accounts of her unusual spiritual experiences as a child. At ages three and four, she loved to lie outside at night on a blanket looking up at the stars. She spent time talking to the clouds. She directed the clouds to move with her mind, and they would. She talked to her brothers about this. They couldn't move the clouds, but they saw she could. By this time, the veil had come down, and Marla was no longer a conscious being. However, she still had many of the abilities from when she was conscious.

At this young age, Marla could also communicate with the trees and nature. She had an awareness she was one with the trees. They did not give guidance or speak to her in words. She simply *knew* she was one with them; she felt this way about all trees. They were like a loved one or a parent to her. She remembers spending a lot of time alone with the trees and nature. As an adult, she still loves to walk in the woods, and she still has relationships with the trees.

As a child, Marla was obsessed with trying to levitate and moving things with her mind. She had a memory of being able to do both of these at some previous time. It seemed normal to her. Of course, she was totally frustrated she couldn't do it now. She also started drawing triangles at a very early age. She drew pages and pages of triangles. This was a memory of knowing sacred geometry in another lifetime. Marla did not understand this connection as a young child. She got the insight about sacred geometry as an adult.

At age five, Marla and a girlfriend were walking home from school. The friend told her to put her tongue on a freezing lamp post. She did, and it hurt really bad when the skin of her tongue stuck to the lamppost. Marla was really hurt and wanted to get back at her little friend. She used the powers of her mind to make her friend fall in a big mud puddle. She immediately felt remorseful and somehow knew this behavior was not in alignment with the good. She knew it was not an arena to play in.

I found it fascinating Marla retained these abilities from past lives even though the veil of forgetfulness came down at age three, and she was no longer a conscious being. My intuition says Marla, like so many other spiritual healers, unconsciously brings in healing techniques she knew from past lives when she was also a spiritual healer.

SPIRITUAL DISCUSSION

It's very unusual for a person to be born conscious in the womb. I've never had another client describe this experience during a regression session. I'm sure there are other evolved human beings here on Planet Earth; however, I have not had the privilege of meeting them.

Marla's story provides us with a case where the adopted baby has no prenatal wounding. In this scenario, the baby came in with no veil between her human consciousness and her soul consciousness. **Therefore, she could remember creating her soul plan before coming to Earth.** The plan was to be born to one mother and then be placed with another family chosen by her soul. Consequently, this adopted baby had no soul wound over leaving her birth mother and going to a different family. Obviously, this can happen, but it's extremely rare.

Marla has fulfilled the soul purpose she discovered during her regression. Throughout her whole life she has served humanity with her gift of healing, and she has devoted her life to relieving the suffering of those here on Planet Earth. Marla is dedicated to keeping her vibrational frequency at a very high level so she can keep enhancing her skills as a healer, psychic/medium, and a clairvoyant. This is not an easy task. To achieve this goal, she is totally disciplined about her lifestyle. She eats only organic food, meditates hours each day, avoids alcohol, caffeine, meat, and all animal products. She has also disciplined her mind to hold positive thoughts and keep her focus on gratitude. In addition, Marla chooses to spend time with like-minded spiritual people.

Obviously, Marla is a highly evolved soul. She came in as a radiant baby years before I even coined the term. She is a forerunner of how humankind will be in the future. As mass consciousness evolves, and humankind becomes more enlightened, there will be more and more people who, like Marla, are conscious while in the womb. As these special beings grow to adulthood, they will hold that state of consciousness where there is no veil between the Spirit World and the earthly world. Remember Marla's channeled message from Chapter One:

> *These babies will come in with a frequency that is higher than our regular people here on Planet Earth. They will carry the high, high frequencies of the Masters. They will become the spiritual teachers of the future. They will change our planet to a place that is peaceful, loving, and harmonious. This large group of souls have all volunteered to save the planet in this way.*

A very important part of my soul purpose is to bring in the radiant babies who will be like Marla. They will also be conscious beings in the womb, and they will be born without a veil that blocks the knowledge of coming from the light and having a soul plan. These babies are coming to help the world evolve. It is all meant to be. It is all part of a grand soul plan for Planet Earth. It gives me great joy to know my soul planned to be part of this grand plan.

Chapter Summary

The stories in this Adoption Chapter illustrate how regressing back into the womb and viewing the soul journey to Earth with soul eyes, allows for profound healing of this deep wound called soul loss. This is my unspoken expectation for each healing session with clients who have been placed for adoption. I expect each client to have a direct experience of the Light of God and to receive visions that come directly from their own soul. Sending the energy of Divine Light/Love into the client's heart opens the door for their soul to bring the visions of what was happening at the soul level. This experience creates the space for the miracle of healing soul loss.

In the case of adoption, the deepest healing happens when the adopted person makes a spiritual connection with the soul of the birth mother and feels the energy of her soul love even for a few seconds. The regressed adult often announces: "She loves me! I can feel it." It's this experience of soul love that shifts the consciousness of each regressed client. Now this person can believe: *My mother truly loved me, and I am lovable.* This shift is life changing.

This soul connection with the mother is present in the adoption stories for David, Lily, and Debbie. Marla didn't need it because she was conscious in the womb and knew her birth mother was only a surrogate.

I trust the clients in this chapter were guided by Spirit to connect with me so they could heal the soul wound created by their adoption. They were drawn to me by an invisible magnetic force. My soul plan calls for me to do this work. Their soul plan included a soul lesson of healing the soul loss of their adoption. It was all meant to be.

CHAPTER FIVE

MY GRANDMOTHER STORY

The Announcement Dream

I woke in the middle of the night startled by a dream. I could feel the energy of joy and excitement flowing through my heart. I knew I had just come back from a journey out into the Universe, but the content of the dream eluded me. Slowly the dream flowed into my consciousness and jolted me even more awake.

In the dream I was having a conversation with my son. It was very strange because I had this split screen of consciousness. He was home in his kitchen in Utah talking on the phone to me. I was home in Indiana having a phone conversation with him. At the same time, I was floating above his kitchen looking down on the scene as he talked with me. It was a very cool perspective, to say the least. In the dream my son said, "Hey, Mom. Did you know Jackie's pregnant?"

That was the message that startled me awake. I was filled with such joy knowing my daughter was pregnant with her first child. Truly, I felt my soul energy flowing into my heart and lighting up my whole being. I held my heart and burst into tears of joy. This was no ordinary dream. It was an announcement dream alerting me to the arrival of a soul coming to join our family. I felt so blessed to understand the significance of this message from Spirit.

I felt my son's message was meant just for me. It was not something I should broadcast to friends and family. So, I decided to keep this announcement dream my own little secret I could hold in my heart until my daughter was ready to share her news. I spoke not a word to anyone. As I went about my life, I felt my own heart expanding to hold all the love I felt for this soul who was coming to be my precious grandbaby.

I immediately started meditating and doing the Radiant Baby Process for my daughter. Every morning I took 15 to 20 minutes to visualize sending Divine Light from my heart to my daughter's womb. I was in Indiana, and she lived in Chicago, but I knew the distance didn't matter. I imagined myself sitting right next to her with my hands on her belly sending the Divine Light and messages of love to this precious baby.

This soul came from Heaven and was swimming in a sea of Divine Light before making the journey to Earth. I wanted this incoming soul to feel *I'm home* while developing a tiny baby body within my daughter's womb. I knew filling my daughter's womb with the light would accomplish this goal. I also knew this soul was meant to be a radiant baby.

This was such a special time for me. Those 15 minutes of sending Divine Light to my daughter's womb became the highlight of each day. I knew I was raising my own vibratory frequency and expanding my aura while doing the visualizations. Joy filled my whole being every morning, knowing my grandbaby would be swimming in a sea of Divine Light/Love while in her mother's womb.

I also had a bit of sadness because I couldn't share this journey with my daughter. She was 36 years old at this stage in her life. She didn't hold my beliefs about spiritual healing and birthing radiant babies. I gently reminded myself I had not experienced my own spiritual awakening at that age either.

I patiently waited for Jackie to announce her pregnancy. I had the dream in August, so I expected her to share her news within three months. We went through Thanksgiving with nothing. Then we went through Christmas with nothing. Each family gathering, I waited, appearing outwardly calm while inside I was quite agitated and went home each time with a heavy heart. I began to doubt my intuitive knowing about this baby coming to our family. However, I continued to send the Divine Light/Love every morning, without fail.

While this was going on with my daughter and her possible pregnancy, another story was unfolding in the family. In February, my 84-year-old mother was admitted unconscious to our local hospice facility. She fell into a coma at home and was not expected to regain consciousness. Amazingly, she was in the coma for three weeks and then woke up with all her mental faculties. The doctors called it a miracle.

On Saturday I called my daughter to say, "Your grandmother is awake."

She said, "OK. Then we'll come visit tomorrow. Can you be there?"

"Of course," I answered.

Her tone of voice left me wondering. *Was she finally going to make an announcement about this incoming baby?* By this time, it was six months since my prophetic dream.

What unfolded next was a scene forever etched in my memory. Jackie and her husband stood on one side of the bed with me on the other side. Jackie was holding her grandmother's hand when she said, "We're so happy you're awake. We have some exciting news to tell you. We're going to have a baby girl in August! We wanted to wait until we were three months along before sharing our news."

My mother didn't miss a beat. She responded with tears in her eyes, "How wonderful! I had two baby girls in August some 60 years ago." This was true; she wasn't in a state of confusion. My mother had twin girls in August, and I was one of those twins.

My heart burst with such joy to finally get this announcement. The proud parents and I were all hugging and crying and laughing at the same time while my mother looked on. Then I quickly did the math. I had the dream three months before this baby was even conceived. And I'd been sending the light ever since. So now we had six more months before this precious baby would be born. Of course, there was no question. I knew I would be sending the light to this baby girl every day for the next six months.

I stepped back and observed my pregnant daughter talking with her grandmother. Here we were—four generations of women gathered together in my mother's room at a hospice center. The oldest, the family matriarch, had little time left here on this Earth. It was obvious her soul was calling her home. At the same time, another beautiful soul was making the journey to Earth and adding another generation to our family.

I found myself holding opposing feelings within my heart. I was filled with sadness about my mother leaving and at the same time filled with joy about this incoming soul. It was a lot to hold. This swirl of emotions must have opened my heart and opened a channel to my higher self. I heard the whispering voice of my soul say:

> *The family pattern of prenatal wounding will stop with the birth of this incoming soul!*

This awareness came into my consciousness like a lightning bolt. It took my breath away and made me dizzy. I was bowled over with the knowledge of what was happening for our family at the spiritual level. I felt the enormity of changing this ancestral pattern that probably went back even more generations than I knew. I was filled with gratitude for all the human beings and spirit beings who assisted me on my journey to identify, heal, and prevent prenatal wounding.

I can identify at least three generations of prenatal wounding in my own family. My mother had prenatal wounding because she was conceived just months after her older brother was killed in an accident. So, my mother was surrounded with the energy of grief the whole time she was in the womb. I suffered the same prenatal wounding when my mother couldn't bond with me while I was in the womb. Then I continued the pattern with my daughter because I was deeply depressed while she was developing in my womb. Of course, this pattern of prenatal wounding was happening outside our awareness. We couldn't prevent or change what we didn't know. I have an intuitive sense it was all meant to be just the way our lives unfolded. We each were learning our soul lessons and fulfilling the soul contracts we made before coming to Earth.

My mother passed just weeks after knowing her great granddaughter was joining the family. I often think she woke up from her coma just so she could share in the joy about this baby girl. Then another little miracle happened. Spirit gifted me with a vision during my mother's funeral service. There was my mother on the other side, alive and well and glowing in a sea of Divine Light. She was holding a little baby girl! My mother was able to hold this baby, soul to soul, before any of us were able to hold her in the physical. Tears of joy flowed down my face. This vision was such a gift!

The next six months I continued to do my morning meditation of sending Divine Light to my daughter's womb. Now I no longer had to wonder if she was really pregnant. I could imagine a beautiful baby girl absorbing the light in all the cells of her little baby body. I was at the hospital when my grandbaby slipped from her mother's womb into this world. She was born with big bright eyes and a big bright aura that extended way out from her body. Her parents named her Melissa. As I held Melissa to my heart, a whispering voice from within conveyed this message: *This is a Radiant Baby. All is as it was meant to be.*

This story doesn't end with Melissa's birth. When she was an infant, I often laid her on my chest after filling my heart with Divine Light/Love. Then I placed my hands on the back of her little heart and made a cocoon with the Divine Love energy. She sank into my chest and laid there limp as could be—absorbing all the love energy. She wouldn't move for two hours at a time. I held sacred space without saying a word, and she too lay absolutely quiet. I couldn't see her little eyes because she always turned her head to the side. My husband was often at the other end of the couch watching TV. I waved at him and mouthed the words, "Is she asleep?" He shook his head and whispered, "Nope, eyes wide open."

For the first year of her life, I held my precious grandbaby and allowed her to sink into my chest. These are some of the most profound spiritual experiences of my life. Each time I could feel the God-energy fill my heart and light up the whole room. I often felt our hearts melting together and becoming one. Sometimes I could even sense our auras merging and creating a feeling of oneness. We literally blissed out. It was like meditating together if you can imagine an infant having the ability to meditate. While our physical bodies relaxed on the couch, I received visions of our spirit bodies dancing and spinning in the light. We were two beings of light swirling higher and higher out in the Universe. **So, we danced soul to soul to the music of the angels.**

DEVELOPING RADIANT HEART HEALING

Radiant Heart Healing came to me as a gift from Spirit in August, 1984. It flowed in unbidden on the wings of Grace, causing my own spiritual awakening and a profound transformation of my work as a psychotherapist. For the past 36 years since its arrival, I have humbly trusted the process and observed this precious gift as it developed over time. What has evolved is a healing process that assists people to awaken to Spirit, raise their vibratory frequencies, and live at higher levels of consciousness. I guide each soul to transform their life tragedy into a journey of spiritual evolution. **This is the key element of Radiant Heart Healing.**

The First Radiant Heart Healing Session

When I founded my holistic health center in 1984, I had no awareness of spiritual healing, chakras, auras, Reiki, or spirit communication. Within months, Spirit sent a husband-wife team who were both Reiki Master Practitioners. Intuitively, I hired them and began learning about spiritual healing.

Weeks later I was dealing with a very suicidal client. The plan was for this client to get three back to back sessions: massage, followed by Reiki, and psychotherapy with me. The goal was to get the re-decision, *I want to live.* I walked into the room where my client was lying on her back on a massage table. I bent over the table to hold her in a hug. She went into deep crying. When she could catch her breath she announced, **"My chest, my chest, feels filled up for the first time in my life!"** As I continued to hold her, she shifted into joyous laughter and announced, **"I want to live!"**

I came to understand this miracle of transformation was caused by a transference of Divine Love. It occurred by accident while I held this client heart to heart. Immediately, I set an intention to get this transference of Divine Love energy to happen by design. The result of that intention has been a Spirit guided journey to create Radiant Heart Healing. It's a journey that is still evolving as I write this book 36 years later.

When our hearts are radiant, meaning open and filled with Divine Love, we are spiritually awake and connected to our souls. Those who achieve a state of radiance are more intuitive, creative, passionate about life, and living their spiritual purpose. We are all born to be radiant. However, most people go through life with their hearts closed by the pain of unhealed childhood emotional wounds. I work in partnership with each client and Spirit to iden-tify and heal old emotional energies that block their hearts. Then we use visualizations to fill their hearts with Divine Love. The goal of each session is to forge a connection to the client's spiritual nature and allow healing to flow from their soul.

Radiant Heart Healing can be used to clear many issues includ-ing prenatal wounding. Using this spiritual process, clients can open to soul love, attain forgiveness, build more loving relationships, and learn the soul lessons they came to Earth to learn this lifetime.

Spirit Beings Appear in My Healing Sessions

Most of the stories in this book involve the presence of spirit beings—angels, the spirits of loved ones, the spirit of a vanishing twin, Mother Mary, Archangel Michael, and many others. As the reader, you may find this difficult to accept, especially if you've not had your own experience of a spiritual vision or a message from Spirit. More than half of the people who have lost a loved one experience some kind of communication from the spirit of that loved one. It's much more common than you think because most people keep their spiritual experiences a secret. They don't want anyone to make fun of their sacred experience or define them as crazy.

When doing healing sessions, I intentionally hold sacred space for the client. Before each session, I fill my healing room with Divine Light and invite all my spiritual helpers to be present. I do this knowing they will inspire me to find the key for healing each person, and guide the words I say to each client. Sensitive people, who feel energy, often tell me it feels like a church in my healing room. They also report getting goose bumps when walking into my healing space. Working in a space filled with such a high frequency allows the client to heal at a deeper level.

I have a gift for working with people who have never before had a spiritual experience. In each healing session, I use the Radiant Heart Healing guided imagery to open their hearts, release the energy of emotional pain, and then fill their hearts with the energy of Divine Love. I deliberately assist them in raising their vibration, so they can ascend into the light. Most clients spontaneously open to seeing the Divine Light that flows into the room, and many are gifted with visions from the Spirit World.

I'm always thrilled when my client has a visitation from an angel, Mother Mary, a spirit baby, or the spirts of loved ones. The visions come directly to my clients as opposed to coming to me. It's usually a dramatic surprise to the client, but it's no surprise to me because of my 36 years of experience with this work.

I personally have had visions of spirit beings since 1980. My dear mother-in-law appeared as a spirit in my living room two days after her funeral. She materialized looking young, beautiful, whole, and radiant after dealing with cancer. Divine Light radiated from her face and her chest. She looked like herself, and at the same time, she looked like an angel. It was a transformational moment for me. In a flash, I knew without even thinking about it—there is no death. My dear Golda is alive and well in a place of light. It's a place I can only visit when I raise my vibration high enough to also be in the light. When she appeared, I was deep in meditation—that's what allowed this miracle to occur.

This experience was the catalyst for me to study spirit communication and the afterlife. I had an inner drive to understand the miracle that happened to me. Golda's visitation was the catalyst that changed my personal life and my professional life. Before this experience, I kept my focus on the material world, being a wife and mother, teaching math, and creating a home. Golda's appearance opened me to a whole new world—a world of seeing the Divine Light, healing with hands-on energy work, and connecting with spirit beings.

GLOSSARY OF TERMS

Chakra

Chakra is a word from India meaning "spinning wheel of light." This light is divine energy. It enters humans from the crown of their heads and travels down through their body in a series of interconnected wheels of energy called chakras. This is how divine energy is distributed throughout the body. There are seven of these main energy centers along the spine. People with the gift of spiritual sight can see them.

Clairvoyant

Clairvoyance means "clear seeing" which refers to psychic seeing. People who have this gift might see flashes of light and color, floating orbs in the space around them, or a glowing light around people. They also might see spirit loved ones, angels, or other mystical visions. Some exceptional children report such experiences as soon as they can communicate. Some people open to this spiritual gift later in life after learning to meditate or having a near death experience.

Death Wish

A death wish is a desire to leave the planet and go to the light on the other side. It can be conscious or unconscious. People with prenatal wounding often create a death wish in the womb.

Divine Light

Divine Light is the Light of God. It's called by many different names such as Holy Spirit, God's healing energy, and the Light of Christ. People who have a near-death experience cross over into Heaven and come back to describe this incredible light that is brighter than any light ever experienced here on Earth. Spirit beings often appear in visions with this Divine Light glowing from within. Spiritual healers are trained to connect with this Divine Light that fills the Universe, bring it through their heart, and send it out their hands into their clients to create a shift and raise the client's vibratory frequency. This Divine Light promotes the healing of everything including emotional trauma and physical issues.

Divine Love

Divine Light is what we see, and Divine Love is what we feel when this Divine Light is present. The experience of Divine Love is very hard to describe. There are no words to adequately express the wonderous, all-encompassing feeling of God's love. Some people who have a near death experience describe feeling uplifted, filled with forgiveness, surrounded by compassion, and a feeling of oneness with every living thing in the world. Having an encounter with a Spirit Being can also create the same feeling. For most people the experience of Divine Love is life changing.

Divine Light/Love

I coined the term Divine Light/Love. The Divine Light is what we *see* and Divine Love is what we *feel*. When a person sees the

Divine Light, he automatically feels the Divine Love. Using the term Divine Light/Love reflects the idea that seeing the light and feeling the light happen simultaneously.

Hathor Angels

The Hathor Angels are part of the ancient Egyptian culture. They are a group of high frequency spiritual beings who are much like the Archangels in our culture. The Hathors show themselves to clairvoyants as 12 feet tall golden angels. Many believe the Hathor Angels created the healing ceremonies used in the Healing Temples of Isis. Many spiritual healers receive clairvoyant visions of these powerful golden angels.

Healing Back in Time

Using guided imagery, the client is directed to visualize a positive womb experience which then replaces their memory of the original womb experience.

Healing Touch

This is another form of spiritual healing that involves working with the person's energy field to clear blocks and promote soul energy flowing easily through the body. Many nurses are currently certi-fied as Healing Touch Practitioners.

Holding Sacred Space

Holding sacred space means the healing practitioner keeps the energy in the room at a high frequency through prayer, visualiz-ing Divine Light in the room, or inviting spiritual helpers such as Christ, Mother Mary, angels or spirit loved ones to be present and interact in the session. When I hold sacred space, I become very quiet and essentially turn the session over to Spirit. I often invite spirit beings to bring messages directly to my client. These messages always contain spiritual wisdom and guidance that is more enlightening than anything I might say to the client.

Human Eyes

This term refers to seeing the world through our physical eyes and seeing only a five-sense reality.

Life Wish

A life wish is a strong desire to live life with passion and joy.

Light Worker

A light worker is a person who uses Divine Light to create healing for self and/or others. There are many, many different healing modalities that use this Divine Light. Reiki and Healing Touch are two examples. Radiant Heart Healing is also a method of spiritual healing that uses the power of the Divine Light. So, I consider myself a light worker. My students certified in Radiant Heart Healing are also considered light workers.

Master Teachers

The term master teachers refers to spirit beings who exist in the Divine Light and send Divine Love and spiritual guidance to Earth so human beings can become more enlightened. Christ, Mother Mary, Buddha, and Mohammad are just a few examples of these Master Teachers.

Radiant Heart Healing

Radiant Heart Healing is a new model of spiritual healing gifted to Dr. Sharon Wendt Wesch in 1984. The simple formula for this method is: 1) open the heart and release the human pain 2) fill the heart with the energy of Divine Love. 3) Hold sacred space for the client to have a shift in consciousness. The high frequency energy of Divine Light/Love creates the healing.

Prenatal Regression Therapy

Using a gentle hypnosis technique, an adult client can go back into the womb and access the baby's sensations, thoughts, and feelings that are now held in the unconscious mind.

Reiki Healing

Reiki is a Japanese form of energy healing brought to the United States in the early 1940s. Reiki helps people with both physical and emotional pain, sleep issues, and invites a spiritual awakening for the client. Many nurses trained in Reiki Healing provide healing sessions for patients in hospitals and outpatient sessions.

Sacred Space

Sacred space can be a place of prayer or a place where ancient spiritual rituals have been performed for centuries. It can also be a physical space such as a healing room that is cleared of negativity and purposely filled with Divine Light/Love and angels so the frequency in the room is very high. Spiritual healing is easier to accomplish in such a high frequency environment.

Soul Eyes

With their physical eyes closed, people can 'see' in their mind's eye. They receive visions of high frequency spiritual energy such as Divine Light, the auras around people, spirits of loved ones, angels, and spiritual teachers such as Christ and Mother Mary. These spiritual images are not seen by people using their human eyes.

Soul Plan

There is a metaphysical theory that before coming to Earth each soul makes a plan for their life that includes difficulties to overcome (soul lessons) and a spiritual purpose or mission to be accomplished. The plan also includes gifts and talents the souls bring in order to accomplish their mission. Souls create a plan to experience prenatal wounding to learn important soul lessons such as: *I am lovable, I was born exactly the way my soul chose for me*, or *I want to live*. After coming to Earth, the soul plan, soul lessons, and soul mission are held in the person's unconscious. The journey of spiritual awakening often brings the soul plan to conscious awareness.

The soul plan holds the premise: *My soul chose this birth scenario so I could learn my soul lessons and achieve great soul growth. My soul wants me to heal my suffering, give up my victim consciousness, and feel empowered to create a life filled with peace, love, and joy.* My clients usually feel empowered when they embrace the idea that their very own soul created the soul plan they are now living.

Grand Soul Plan

Each individual soul has a unique soul plan. Likewise, large groups of souls such as an extended family or a nation can have a grand soul plan that includes the interactions and relationships of souls within a group. I believe Spirit has a Grand Soul Plan to bring in radiant babies at this time on Planet Earth. I am only one soul committed to this plan. There are many, many other healers, parents, and incoming babies who are also part of this Grand Soul Plan.

Source

Source is simply another word for God.

Spirit

Spirit is also another word for God or Universal Love. The Native Americans used the term Great Spirit to refer to an energy force that brings life to all human beings and all living creatures, including trees and plants. They prayed to their Great Spirit and believed their prayers were answered.

CPSIA information can be obtained
at www.ICGtesting.com
Printed in the USA
LVHW021151230121
677173LV00003B/219